NEAR AND DISTANT HORIZONS:

IN SEARCH OF
THE PRIMARY SOURCES
OF KNOWLEDGE

JOHN HERLIHY

NEAR AND DISTANT HORIZONS

IN SEARCH OF THE PRIMARY SOURCES OF KNOWLEDGE

SOPHIA PERENNIS

HILLSDALE NY

Second Edition, Sophia Perennis, 2005
First Edition, Writers Club Press
an imprint of iUniverse.com, Inc., 2000

Series editor: James R. Wetmore

For information, address:
Sophia Perennis, P.O. Box 611
Hillsdale NY 12529
sophiaperennis.com

Printed in the
United States of America

Library of Congress Cataloging-in-Publication Data

Herlihy, John
Near and distant horizons : in search of the
primary sources of knowledge / Herlihy, John—2nd ed.

p. cm.
Includes bibliographical references.
ISBN 1 59731 002 6 (pbk: alk. paper)
ISBN 1 59731 008 5 (cloth: alk. paper)
1. God (Islam)—Knowableness. 2. Creation (Islam). 3. Evolution—Religious
aspects—Islam. 4. Philosophy, Islamic. I. Title.
BP 166.2.H47 2004
297.2—dc22   2004025035

CONTENTS

DEDICATED TO
DR MOHSEN AL-LABBAN

He lifts the veil and shows the way

☾ ☾ ☾

FOREWORD

THE QUESTION OF PRIMARY SOURCES

WE HAVE UNDERTAKEN THIS INQUIRY into the Islamic sources of traditional knowledge because their value and validity have been seriously undermined during these times by the predominant worldview of modern science. The scientific paradigm of knowledge denies the existence of other levels of reality and does not recognize the validity of revelation, the significance of nature, and the importance of *Homo sapiens* as a being created as a human likeness of the divine prototype of God. As a result, many sincere people who would otherwise preserve a firm faith in God seriously doubt the validity of these sources of knowledge as a frame of reference and question their effectiveness as a guide for ethical action. Instead of confronting the challenges and hardships of life with a traditional doctrine concerning the origin, purpose and final end of existence, the great unsolved mysteries confronting humanity are the subject of endless speculation and a fundamental ignorance now prevails concerning the knowledge and wisdom that has uplifted traditional peoples down through the ages.

The question of primary sources and the authenticity of knowledge are vital to the life of our time. Never before has so much discredit been cast upon the traditional knowledge embedded within the revelations and sacred myths that substantiate the great world religions. Moreover, an expression of perennial doubt persists within the scientific community itself that filters down into the mentality of the mass population, questions concerning the unresolved antagonism that exists between the encounter and interface of religion and science. Scientists are even questioning the potential limits of science and speak of the end of physics, while certain key scientific theories, such as the origin of the universe, the origin of life and our own human origins are now openly admitted to be 'unique events' that cannot be subjected to any experimental investigation and therefore can never, according to the scientific mandate, be subject to scientific validation.

This preface asks a number of questions that the rest of the book hopes to answer. What are the primary sources of knowledge? Are they valid, authentic and objective beyond any reasonable human doubt? Is there a headwater of knowledge or a well-spring of truth that serves as the fundamental source of all knowing, or is knowledge relative and all truth conditioned by the impulses of human minds such as contemporary scientists would have us believe? Is there a source so far beyond the edge and so transcending that it has the power to wipe away all duality and all polarity, a mega-power that is able to synthesize into a single unifying web the disparate elements that we witness within the existential reality of our lives? In short, is there a knowledge that can neutralize the split image of the horizon and bring the multifarious elements of the phenomenal world into a unified Whole?

When it comes to the question of a knowledge that explains certain fundamental mysteries, a knowledge that transcends any 'provable' medium such as the alleged objectivity of matter, and a knowledge that rises above the level of pure reasoning to the realm of ultimate meaning and purpose, the subject of sources and their authenticity must inevitably arise and be seriously considered. It does not matter to what extent we as a civilization are able to uncover aspects of a knowledge that may lead to the explanation of certain fundamental mysteries. What must sustain a viable credibility in the minds and hearts of mass populations around the globe will be the original sources of a particular paradigm of knowledge and the authenticity of its consequent worldview. Ultimately, the only thing that truly matters to humankind is whether the knowledge of the absolute Reality is true and whether it lives in the mind as an enduring certainty.

Two fundamental considerations form the underlying ground of this work and we will state them clearly now since there is no other reason for writing this book. The first consideration touches upon the kind of knowledge that we seek because humans are born to 'know' and their true vocation is the pursuit of a knowledge they can experience and live by. The second consideration is born of the first by asking what the source of our knowledge is and from whence does it derive its principial quality and its certitude. Are there headwaters for the laws and principles that flow through the cosmos into the human mind? Is there a wellspring of knowledge that shrouds in a perennial mystery our human origins and the birth of the universe that seals with certainty our meaning and the ultimate fulfillment of the creation?

We intend to answer these questions by referring to the three clearly articulated sources of knowledge as they are identified within the religion of Islam, namely Revelation as the divine disclosure of the Mind of God, Nature as the naturalized and formal body of God and Humankind as the human likeness of God. Stephen Hawkins, the well-known and controversial physicist, concluded his intriguing book *A Brief History of Time* with two surprising aspirations, firstly to discover a complete theory of knowledge concerning the true nature of reality whose broad principle could be understood by everyone, and secondly to understand why we exist within this universe. 'For then,' he concludes, 'we would know the mind of God.' For a contemporary scientist, it is a bold and courageous thought. From the traditional Islamic point of view, however, the mind of God has already been made manifest through the verses of sacred Quranic scripture and the other traditionally accepted revelations down through the millennia.

The Quran itself is, of course, the primary source of knowledge *par excellence* within the Islamic tradition and a sacred communication from the Mind of God to the mind of man. It is the direct descent of the essential knowledge from the Divine Being to the human being through Sacred Speech. The Religion of Islam began as a spiritual force with the first descent of the revelation to the Prophet Mohammed, upon whom blessings and peace, and with the descent of the final verses came the completion and fulfillment of the religion as a spiritual force on earth.

Two other sources of knowledge made available for the benefit of humanity are specifically mentioned in the Quran: 'Soon We will show them Our signs on the horizon and within their own souls, until it becomes clear to them that this is the Truth' (41: 53). These alternative sources of knowledge are respectively the creation in the form of Nature, and the human being who is considered in Islam a living source of knowledge as well as a human revelation. 'Know thyself in order to know thy Lord' is a well-known Holy Tradition (*hadith*) of the Prophet. What may prove enigmatic to the modern mentality, steeped as it is in the secular and scientist ambiance of the modern world, is the meaning of the word 'knowledge' itself, since distinctions need to be made between the sacred and essential knowledge contained within a revealed scripture and the speculative, empirical and scientific knowledge that serves as the backcloth and worldview for the modernist mentality.

Within the Islamic tradition, the Quran clearly states that the source of all true knowledge lies within the phenomenal world as symbolized in the image of the distant horizon and within the human being as symbolized in the image of the near horizon of the self. The near horizon of the inner self lies within and represents a kind of isthmus and passageway between the outer and inner worlds of the mind and heart. The distant earthly horizon marks the terminus of the known world that signifies the end of knowledge and the beginning of mystery. Both horizons imply the possibility of a knowledge that finds its origin in the Absolute Truth and traces its roots back to the Divine Source.

The image of the near horizon within mankind and the distant horizon on the edge of the known world identifies through the bold stroke of a single, horizontal line the separation that exists between two alien worlds, the one physical, visible, and apparently real, the other rarefied, invisible and apparently unreal. The horizon traces the distinct realities of nature and humanity with a celestial line that cuts across the face of the phenomenal world of nature and across the ground of the human soul. On the one side lies the visibly convincing, physical reality of this world, tempting us into believing the world to be an independent reality that is absolute within itself. On the other side lies the elusive world of the spirit that overlays all of physical reality with its vivifying force and its definitive presence.

To look at the distant horizon with its split image of heaven and earth is to gaze at the duality of the world. To gaze at the near horizon that exists within the human being is to bear witness to the duality that exists within us as the existential reality of our being. Heaven and earth, matter and spirit, body and soul, good and evil: These are the existential polarities that highlight the separation of two alien worlds that exist innerly as a near horizon and manifest symbolically on the periphery of the world as the distant horizon. The image of the horizon, as macrocosmic symbol *par excellence*, is the remembrance of the unity of separate worlds that in appearance are two but in truth are one, for as the Quran repeatedly asserts, there is but one Reality and there is only one God.

The split image of the world and the duality within humanity have never held such prominence as during the present era at the dawn of a new millennium. This duality vividly expresses itself during these times in the way we understand ourselves, the way we express our self-image, the way we perceive our world, and the way we approach the very portals of knowledge itself. As individuals, we are living out the complexities of a split image that is embedded within our beings and reflected within the very framework of the creation. Heaven and earth is there on the horizon, as though it were traced across the celestial divide of the heavens with the ink of the Divine Pen. Body, soul and spirit constitute the totality of the human entity, as though the thin line of the near horizon cuts across our being with the invisible blade of the Divinity, thereby creating a clean and unbreachable chasm between the known and unknown self.

This split image of the human being and the world manifests itself during the present era as the relentless influence of the scientific point of view over the minds and hearts of people everywhere. There are now two points of reference and two paradigms of knowledge that vie for the attention of mass populations around the globe. There is the vision of a metaphysical knowledge, of eternal and supernatural realities, that is rooted in first principles and that is conveyed to humanity through revelation, through nature and through ourselves. It is a principial knowledge that begins with revelation, becomes internalized in the mind and heart through faith, and ends with certainty. Then there is the vision of a physical reality, of rational and natural realities rooted in physical matter and conveyed to the human mind through the faculty of reason and the observations and calculations of an experimental and mathematical science. It is a knowledge that begins with hypothesis and ends with the certainty of physical proofs as the definitive source of an objective knowledge and the only reality worth believing in and studying.

The age we live in harbors frightening challenges, but it also inspires bold thinking. There is a feeling of the eleventh hour about our time. Modern speculation concerning the eternal mysteries is fast approaching an edge of time and space whose drop-off point is as abrupt and final as the end of the earth was for 16th century seafarers. Some compensations of this difficult era may provide an unexpected insight into the dilemma that confronts us, but the scientific conception of knowledge has become virtually equated with the only way of knowing there is.

Yet, does this attitude need to set the norm for everyone? People are becoming increasingly aware of how little our rational knowing pushes back the frontiers of our conscious unknowing. What we know no longer begins to satisfy the aching mystery of what we do not know. No matter what wondrous scientific revelation stimulates contemporary thinking—from the theory of relativity to the mysteries of the quantum universe—the parade of demonstrable and ascertainable facts that result from the high fever pursuit of the scientific inquiry throws no more light on the dark mystery that clouds our knowing than a bright wood fire throws into the dark, moonless night.

Yet, there is a way of knowing that transcends the rational world of the mind for a higher consciousness of knowing. Every search implies a journey and every journey requires a final destination. The search for the authentic sources of knowledge begins with the words of revealed scripture, manifests through the symbolic messages of every created thing within the phenomenal world of nature, and ends with the self-revelation of humanity. It marks an inner journey across frontier lands that lie over the border and off the map. No well-defined road leads there and no one can find the way on their own. It is a journey that will take us to the central *mihrab*[1] of the inner self as the focus and prelude for the experience of that

Center and Source of the Metacosmic Universe that exists beyond
the edge of space and time, but that manifests here and now as the
Divine Disclosure and the Sacred Presence.

For these reasons and for others left unstated, we will now pro-
ceed with an inquiry into the Islamic sources of traditional knowledge that has fueled the minds and hearts of men and women down
through the ages and hopefully will continue to do so during the
coming third millennium.

1. Every mosque contains a central prayer niche that faces Makkah and serves
as the orientation point for prayer.

PART A

THE SUPREME MIND OF GOD

When we think of the cosmic universe, what does it mean to us? Do we imagine, for example, dark matter, black holes, and the initial singularity claimed as realities by modern science, or do we envision a universal Creator that lives eternally as the Supreme Intelligence and Absolute Being? Do the laws that govern the ordered cosmos exist as the expression of an inevitable virtuality, or do the natural and universal laws serve as evidence of a Divine Being and reflection of a Supreme Intelligence who created and sustains the universe? How do we know, can we hope to know, will we ever know?

I

FIRST ORIGIN
AND FINAL SOURCE

The knowledge of my Lord encompasses all things (6:80).[1]

WHAT IS KNOWLEDGE? Indeed, what is worth knowing and how do we come to know it? How do we know, for example, that a particular knowledge is authentic and genuinely articulates the truth that we as humans endeavor to uncover and internalize? Does an avowed knowledge offer a convincing explanation of the meaning of humanity and provide a model synthesis concerning the true nature of reality? What are the sources of that knowledge and how do they verify and substantiate what we believe to be true? These are questions that few people consciously ask and that all people will unconsciously answer in one way or another throughout the course of their lives.

The search for the true source of knowledge takes us well beyond ourselves, back to the edge of time and beyond the far side of the horizon, into the cold depths and boundless regions of infinitude and eternity. In order to come to terms with the validity and authenticity of a given paradigm of knowledge, such as traditional or scientific knowledge, we must examine it in the light of its origin and source. With regard to modern science, we do not have far to journey since the scientific approach does not conceptualize the concept of a beginning and end because it cannot fathom the mystery or understand the void that would lie outside the envelope of

---

1. All verses of the Quran are identified in parenthesis by chapter and verse.

the physical world. The origin and source of modern science actually lies within the human being, who relies on the faculty of human reason and the corporeal senses to rationalize and classify the external world in order to witness and objectify what the modern mentality believes to be true. To reach the point of origin with regard to traditional knowledge, we must journey through space and time and distance ourselves from an increasingly complex world environment in order to reach the supreme point of instancy and the profound moment of creation at its absolute source whence arises the wellspring of all knowledge.

When we contemplate the idea of source, the image of the river immediately comes to mind because traditional knowledge is like a moving river that has come down to us in an unbroken current of continuity from time immemorial commencing with the Primordial Tradition. Like a mighty river, such essential knowledge originated at a distinct source and has passed through different landscapes and zones, through diverse epochs and every possible configuration of mind, culture and sensibility, to arrive at the present moment as an eternal offering to humanity from the very fountainhead of life. Like the ever-flowing river, knowledge is a continuity of movement and direction that represents a totality of expression from its first origin to its final destination. Like the river, the current of universal knowledge is definitive and absolute, but it would not exist without the reality of its source, emerging from the very ground of existence by the power of a Supreme Divinity creating a knowledge with a universal meaning and expressing a knowledge of the timeless Reality. If knowledge is a river, then it has sprung from a source that ensures the authenticity and continuity for the articulation of an essential knowledge that is objective and that can provide the framework for the human understanding of the self and the world.

Like the presence of a great river such as the Nile or Ganges, the final source of all traditional knowledge is both sacred and original, sacred because it reflects something infinitely more than itself that it only gradually discloses and manifests; and original, not because it is first or new, but rather because it is a faithful image of the Origin and originates in the One Reality. 'To Him is due the primal origin of the heavens and the earth' (6:101). In the traditional approach, the point of departure in understanding the true nature of reality is generally the same, despite the wide diversity of the religious experience and the historical development of a variety of traditional civilizations. The origin of life and the meaning of existence results from the understanding that the entire creation proceeds from a prime cause or first origin, a cause that is identified as the Transcendent with regard to the unveiling of the creation and the Center with regard to its presence within existence.

Modern science, on the other hand, has its starting point in what amounts to a revolution in human consciousness, a revolution that is an abrupt turning away from the traditional perception of a transcending knowledge that finds its origin and source in the Divine Principle. This revolution of consciousness marks the revolt against Heaven and a turning inward, not through the intelligence of the heart and the emotions of a higher sensibility, but through the purely human faculty of reason, together with a certain logic, that combined with the input of the senses form the *modus operandi* of the scientific method. This approach limits rather than transcends the human perspective by denying *a priori* the authentic sources of knowledge and rejecting the powers of the higher faculties such as intuition and the spiritual instincts such as faith and spiritual sentiment. As a consequence, the conceptions of modern science, relying as they do on the external world of sense-data and sense-impression to establish what constitutes a knowledge of the self and of reality, refers only to what is temporal and finite in the world, and reflects only the logical, mechanical, and 'reasonable' criteria that conform to man's five senses and to human reason.

We are not concerned at this point with either the existence or the definition of traditional knowledge although it forms the texture and frame of which we write; rather we are concerned with clarifying why and how a given body of knowledge, its framework and its ensuing worldview is traditional. The knowledge itself cannot be everything. What makes it anything is the fact that far beyond its actuality lies a source that substantiates it and gives it meaning and life. What makes traditional knowledge unique is the fact that, because of its source within the Divinity, everything within the body of the tradition must already be there from the very beginning, in its essence. The subsequent developments of the tradition and its full articulation, the shades and colors of the traditional knowledge, and the diversity of its scope down through the ages only serve to make it more explicit, without adding new elements from another source. According to the Islamic doctrine, there is only one first origin and final source, namely the knowledge of Unity (*al-Tawhid*) and the knowledge of the One (*al-Ahad*).

We wish to highlight the fact that traditional knowledge is shaped by the nature of its origins and we wish to emphasize the importance of identifying the first principles that form the coloration and ambiance of its enduring truth. The pursuit of knowledge, the recognition of truth and the wisdom of life find their impetus and source within a realm that transcends the temporal and the earthly. It is the sacred realm of universal law, of first principles, of first knowledge and first origins that live now and forever as they exist in truth. It is a realm, needless to say, that originates with He who originates, the First (*al-Awwal*) and the Last (*al-Akhir*). All that we know comes from He who is the Knowing (*al-Alim*), the Living (*al-Hayy*) and the Eternal (*al-Samad*).

The question of the source and authenticity of knowledge that serves as a paradigm of self-knowledge and as a worldview to explain the true nature of the cosmic reality strikes at the heart of the modern understanding of the word *knowledge* and the means of its acquisition. The question of source is fundamental to the entire endeavor in the search for knowledge and will ultimately define the contours, color and shape of any elaborated framework of knowledge whether it is metaphysical, traditional, rational or scientific. The question of the truth of a given framework of knowledge highlights, perhaps more than we may care to admit, the modern-day approach to the search for a unified theory of knowledge that serves as the *raison d'etre* for the scientific enterprise. A comprehensive worldview has the duty to project into the consciousness of the world its objectivity, its persuasiveness, and its validity to the extent that it is accessible and believable to mass populations at its source, is convincing at simple levels of expression, and is profound in its truth.

While no one would deny that a comprehensive knowledge of the reality is of vital interest and importance to humanity and always has been, during these times the modern-day approach and understanding of existential and ultimate knowledge has been two-edged and the search for a complete knowledge runs forward on dual tracks. On the one hand, we have the traditional knowledge that has come down through the millennia and is followed instinctively by billions of people worldwide. Down through the ages, this knowledge has been referred to as higher knowledge, spiritual knowledge, essential knowledge, traditional knowledge and metaphysical knowledge, but it ultimately reflects the instinctive and universal inclination of people in every time and place to resolve their doubts, have faith and believe in God. On the other hand, the defining knowledge of the 20th century is a 'scientific knowledge' that marks the parameters of the contemporary worldview. Alternatively, this knowledge has been referred to as speculative knowledge, rational knowledge, secular knowledge, empirical knowledge, and of course scientific knowledge, but it ultimately reflects a self-proclaimed knowledge in the objectivity of physical matter, rational thinking and mathematical formulation that dominates the intellectual horizon as a sign of our time.

What people yearn for, however, is a definitive knowledge, a principial knowledge and a first knowledge that has the power to resolve the perennial mystery that lies at the heart of existence and at the center of the universe. What we are faced with first and foremost is a mystery rather than a knowledge and what we need to resolve before all else is to know the true origin of existence and have available the true sources of knowledge. At face value, we do not know what constitutes the true nature of the human reality—in terms of first origin or final end—nor do we know what empowers and governs the reality of phenomenal nature that we find within our depths and beyond into the depths of the night sky. At the heart of all existential knowledge lies a divine mystery that declines to give up its secrets and refuses to resolve the enigmatic challenges of life during this or any other time.

To resolve this mystery, the people of more traditional cultures perennially turned to a belief system whose fundamental premises trace their origin and source far beyond the limited borders of the human mentality. They never questioned the knowledge of their otherworldly origin, and they accepted the traditional knowledge concerning the origin of the universe and of life as a revealed truth. This knowledge of origins was clearly disclosed to all traditional peoples through myths, symbols and revelatory scriptures that delineated graphically the creation of the world and of human origins, thus conclusively resolving for them truth's mystery and aligning them with truth's reality. In principle, they lived their lives with a view to the sources of knowledge that were identified and made available to them through their religion and they had available the possibility of incorporating that knowledge into their beings as a realized knowledge.

The universal mystery of life existed for traditional peoples as a truth and its resolution was prefigured in a profound faith in the Supreme Being. In this way, they were able to learn to revere the mystery of life and put away the fear of the unknown just as we have reverence for the coming of the dawn every morning or the descent of night and no more wish to change the rhythm and harmony of these mysteries than we would wish to abandon our faith or alter our cherished beliefs. When we look reflectively at the dark mystery of the night sky and contemplate its overwhelming significance, a new door opens for the human spirit that permits men and women universally to be inexplicably touched by what they gaze upon. For a brief moment, the depths of night provide us with a glimpse of ourselves through the mirror of the deep, dark universe to reveal our world adrift as an island in a stream of stars and galaxies and we upon it as curious pilgrims, voyaging beyond the celestial horizon across a vast sea of space and time. The human mind cannot fathom the broad implications of such a sight, but the human spirit can gaze into this mirror of darkness and see the same truth and the same reality that it witnesses within itself, namely that there is only one Reality and one unifying Truth.

(((

WHEN THE BIBLE refers to a time 'in the beginning', when the Quran identifies the Divine Being with the qualifying names of the First (*al-Awwal*), the Last (*al-Akhir*), the Living (*al-Hayy*) and the Eternal (*al-Samad*), when the traditional literature refers to the Origin and Source of existence and thus a primordial font of all knowledge, these references relate paradoxically to a beginning, an origin and a source that are not in time, but that precede time's commencement, preclude time's final termination, and ultimately transcend time's flowing continuum. The traditional term 'eternal' is not an indefinite duration of lateral time linking past and future or sidereal time determined by the motion of the stars. It is the experience of timelessness itself, the 'eternal now' to which the mystical traditions refer, without the limitations of the spatio-temporal matrix of this world. The Origin and Source do not exist in the past any more than the Final End exists in the future; they both exist in the eternal now as metaphysical realities and divine truths.

That having been said, it is not enough to know that our origins precede us and lead us back to an unspecified moment when something actually had a beginning and began to be. The significance of origin and source actually suggests an orientation, a direction and a moment that is living and eternally real. It cuts through the continuum of time with the vertical axis of the world of the Spirit and comes into temporal existence through a vertical descent that actually pierces the fabric of space and time in order to intersect the horizontal plane of this world with the vertical sword of its decisive and sublime vision.

Both Origin and Source find their substance and meaning in the Absolute, the Supreme Being, and the Existing One or Necessary Existent. Origin refers to the Divinity Who is outside the matrix of a temporal beginning, while Source refers to the Divinity Who is the supreme commander of a universal space that is pre-existent and becomes manifest throughout the universe by the divine act of creation and its subsequent unfolding within time.

God is the ultimate source of all existent things in their multi-faceted manifestations and forms. God, as absolute mystery as well as hidden treasure, is the Originator and Source of all that exists. He is, therefore, the Originator of a time in the beginning, now and ever shall be and He is the Source of all that exists as created and manifested form. Out of the headwaters of the Source flow all primordial forms, all archetypes, all embryos, all seeds, germs, buds, eggs, rootlets, and sprigs. According to Ibn al-'Arabi, buds are possibilities that have not yet 'smelled the perfume of existence.' In the Source, all things are eternally present, just as in the bud the flower is forever ready to become and be. Nothing can appear on the plane of physical manifestation without having its transcendent cause and without the origin of its existence being well placed in the soil of the Primordial Source. Similarly, all existent things both contain and preserve the integrity of the bud, sprig, embryo, seed and source that begot it.

The notion of origin refers to a Supreme Being that is before us, behind us, below us and above us, both now, in the past and in the future, in short in a time that is summarized by the eternal moment. 'It is He who beginneth the process of creation, and He repeateth it' (10:4). The Name of Allah identifies an eternal Presence and a living Reality that is certainly not subject to the conventional notions of time and space. He does not have a beginning in time; instead, He represents the ever-present Origin, Source, Center and Final End. According to a Holy Tradition of the Prophet (*hadith*) in Islam: 'There was a time when God existed, and nothing else existed alongside Him.'

Do we know why the Divinity created the universe? As human beings, we might project anthropomorphic feelings of loneliness in the face of an eternal solitude, but God has revealed another reason. We have come to know why God created the universe because a well-known *hadith qudsi*[2] has conveyed this rarefied knowledge to humanity. 'David (peace be upon him) said, "Oh Lord, why did You cause creation to come into being?" God replied, "I was a hidden treasure and wanted to be known, therefore I created the universe."' We have here in the words of God a direct statement of

---

2. One of the traditional Holy Sayings (*hadith*) of the prophet Mohammed said to be the direct speech of Allah.

divine motivation and purpose that is conveyed to us as a divine disclosure through the prophets so that we may know once and for all time the reason for our existence and the purpose for which we lives, namely to know the Divinity and through the realization of this knowledge to worship and praise Him. The miraculous faculty of consciousness[3] implicit in this revealed knowledge is the counterpart and reflection of the magnificent beauty of the creation.

Evolutionary theory tells us that life emerged upon the earth long ago within the framework of a geologic time in which organic life could evolve because it presumably had eons of time to do so. Similarly, astrophysics leads us back to what scientists call an 'initial singularity', commonly referred to as the Big Bang theory, that occurred some 15 billion years ago, once again allowing for enough time for the earth, the sun, the galaxies and the universe itself to explode out of a compressed point and expand to their present condition.[4] We are not concerned here with a theoretical beginning of the universe any more than we are concerned with the evolutionary progression of life. Within the traditional framework, the origin of the act of creation and its subsequent unfolding can be called an initial singularity without, however, it being an initial moment. In fact, it exists beyond the matrix of space and time within an envelope of metacosmic reality in which the universe itself resides. This reality, the one and only Reality, forms as it were a backcloth upon which the universe rests in cameo.

The act of creation belongs exclusively to the Creator who encompasses the matrix of the universe within His supernal domain. The laws of science would break down at that point in time, so that even if something happened before the event of the creation, science would not be able to say anything about it. According to modern science, events before the Big Bang and therefore

3. Chapter 9 will deal more thoroughly with the significance and implications of man's 'human' consciousness.
4. Scientists are not very exact concerning the origin of time and understandably so. According to Steven Hawking in his *A Brief History of Time* (New York: Bantam Books, 1988), p50, the phenomenon of the Big Bang occurred 'some time in the past (between ten and twenty thousand million years ago), when the density of the universe and the curvature of space-time would have been infinite.'

beyond the horizon of time have no relevance, so they should not be considered a part of any model or theory of the universe. For modern science, time begins with the Big Bang. It speculates no further than that and rightfully so, since the laws of modern science have no jurisdiction beyond that self-appointed moment. That is no justification, however, for claiming much less insisting that nothing exists or happens outside that point in time.

From the traditional point of view, time begins with the origin of the creation, but that does not preclude the existence of the principle of Origin and Originator, which in the Arabic *al-Badi*', is identified in the Quran as one of the 99 names of God. On the contrary, the power of creation belongs to the creating Principle alone. Similarly, the Origin does not mark the genesis of the creation; rather the genesis of creation receives its reality and its truth from the Originator of all things and refers to the Origin for sustenance and support. The meaning of the origin lies in an everlasting beginning that originates outside the cosmos. Time begins in an eternal and ever-present reality, well beyond the reach of modern science. Origin does not begin, rather it exists and is therefore not bound to a space-time continuum. It is not understood to be in time or part of a fixed continuum, rather it partakes of the eternal present and could be identified as a vast mega-universe that constitutes the uncreated milieu of the Divine Spirit.

Ultimately our origin is transcendent and takes root within another dimension of reality. It represents knowledge far beyond the limitations of this world and partakes of the domain of the Spirit. Similarly, our source commences a universal overflowing of the creation, like the overflowing of the Divine Pen[5] that even in exhausting its ink does not exhaust the potential of its words and thus its knowledge. 'Ultimately, the origin is nothing less than the Absolute, the Infinite and Eternal.'[6] As such, our origins still exist; they are ever-present within us; they are always there and always

---

5. If all the trees were pens and all seas were ink with which to record God's speech, they would be exhausted before God's speech runs out' (18:109).

6. Martin Lings, *What is Sufism* (London: George Allen & Unwin, Ltd., 1975), p15.

will be. Because of our origin, we do not live in time; rather time lives in us as a harmonious rhythm of our conscious existence. It flows through us like an advancing river until we die. Then the river flows back into the sea, time terminates for the individual person, and the transcendent soul moves on.

The sense of origin is not something that began in some remote past as a singular and germinal event or as an emerging, molecular thing, that through prolongation, multiplication and advancement evolved into progressive forms of development and arbitrary change, without the subtle implications of the inner envelope of reality. Every created thing exists in principle 'as is' and in its exist-ence always was and always will be. The bud, the seed, the egg and the root all contain the origin within them, just as the river contains the source, and this truth permits them to exist and function according to what they are in principle. All things suffer birth, growth, maturity, decline, and death on an individual and formal basis, but on a universal and spiritual basis, they transcend time and partake of eternity because of the truth of the Origin and the Source that lies within everything as a living reality and an eternal truth.

To have faith in a body of traditional knowledge and to live a tra-ditional life of spirituality is to live within sight of the Origin. It is because of the origin of existence and the sources of knowledge that every moment of life can be lived at all, giving life its spiritual and transcendent character. Those who deny this deny the living reality within themselves. Those who experience this live a life of affirma-tion that finds its source and origin in the Divine Being who is the Creator and Originator of the space-time matrix that characterizes the universal cosmos.

(((

THE CONCEPT OF THE SOURCE conjures up a number of primor-dial images that continue to inspire the human imagination. We have suggested that the origin creates, and perpetually re-creates in remembrance, the dawn of the creation and the origin of life. If Origin is cosmic genesis, then Source feeds the headwaters of the universe, the springs of life and the fountains of knowledge. We place our roots into the primordial source of existence because the flow of its headwaters, springs and fountains nourish our consciousness with a spiritual identification with all that is, has been, or ever could be.

> What is drawn back by spiritual realization towards the Source might be called the centre of consciousness. The Ocean is within as well as without; and the path of the mystics is a gradual awakening as it were 'backwards' in the direction of the root of one's being, a remembrance of the Supreme Self which infinitely transcends the human ego and which is none other than the Deep towards which the wave ebbs.[7]

The point of departure is beyond time, space and any potential configuration of thought within the human mind left solely to its own devices.

When the religions, Islam in particular, mention the way of return, they are referring to a return in the direction of the Source from which all things originate. The way of return represents the harmonious conditioning of both origin and source within our lives as a conscious and living reality, and not as a return backwards or movement forwards since our origin and source transcend time and space as an eternal presence. This living reality leads upward on the vertical axis in order to surpass the individual self for the greater Self that lies beyond the near horizon of the soul.

> Only if we recognize the past as a 'true dimension of ourselves,' and not only as an abstract property of time, shall we be able to see ourselves in proper perspective to the universe, which is not an alien element that surrounds us mysteriously, but the very body of our past, in whose womb we dream until we awake into the freedom of enlightenment.[8]

This vertical axis comes into existence through a vertical descent

---

7. Ibid., p13.

8. Lama Govinda, *Creative Meditation and Multi-Dimensional Consciousness* (Wheaton, IL: Quest Books, 1976), p266.

that actually pierces the fabric of space and time in order to intersect the horizontal plane within this world at every point in time
with elements of the Eternal and the Infinite.

Every spiritual tradition begins at a mythical pre-dawn, a beginning that represents the true origin of life and the source of all
knowledge and action. To return to our origin is to return to our
spiritual roots, when the Origin is eternally fresh and the Source is
forever near. To return to the source is to return to the primordial
condition of humanity, which means a return to the state of a
human perfection that is prefigured in primordiality and will come
to fulfillment in the paradise, but that exists as an archetype in the
continuity of the timeless Origin. To remember our origins and to
keep faith within the source of all existence represent a progressive
awakening that forms the basis of the earthly journey and the framework of the spiritual ascent.

Every spiritual tradition germinates and comes to fruition in the
reality of the soul. Human beings exist, live, and breathe because of
the reality of their souls whose existence begins with Source and
finds its final consummation in the abiding Spirit. Referring to the
source is referring first to the existence of our individual soul and by
extension the spirit that animates that soul with the Breath (*al-
nafas*) of the Divine. The great paradox of the modern age is that
our inward reality—our consciousness—is the only thing we do
know in certitude, and our knowledge is not scientific or rational
but spontaneous and intuitive, providing us with the only existential certainty worth having faith in. We can be in doubt about our
sense perception and in dispute over outward things and their rela-
tionships, but our own existence can cause no suspicion of doubt at
the risk of giving up the overwhelming reality of consciousness. The
seemingly unreal inner reality of our being which we cannot see and
modern science cannot verify proves to be the one reality worth
believing in.

Traditional peoples understood the importance of the 'inward
reality'. They understood implicitly that it is not enough to see
as humans see, even if it means that they can devise microscopes
and telescopes that can see into the heart of the microbe and the
distant regions of the universe. Traditional peoples never permitted

themselves to be content with sensory knowledge and its extensions to satisfy the deep and fundamental yearning to know the ultimate potential as well as the true nature of the reality we experience so clearly in its three dimensional and physical aspect. Modern and contemporary people are satisfied with what are but the external appearances of things and their surface impressions. What things are in their living reality is something that does not interest the denizens of modern science and can never be substantiated by human reason and the senses alone.

Still, if our knowledge is superficial today because of the modern scientific obsession with physical matter and its attempt to quantify the external reality without recognizing the quality of the inward reality, it is also dangerous because the balance that once existed during the traditional times in allowing for a supernatural basis for the physical reality is gone, a balance needless to say that was reflected in all aspects of life. We move about the earth with unprecedented speed, but we do not know where we are going or whether we shall find happiness once we get there. We have accumulated vast amounts of information and through the technology of the Internet can transmit the data around the globe at the speed of light, and yet we do not know who we are and how we should live.

If we have learned nothing else from the developments of the 20th century, perhaps we should now accept and internalize the following insight. No factual and scientific knowledge we now know or stand to learn in the future will bring us any closer to whom we are and what we need to accomplish in the totality of our beings. It is not enough to split the atom into a million subatomic particles, for we have learned that it carries the risk of being confronted with a contradiction that could undermine the foundation of the modern scientific worldview.[9] It is not enough to be able to manipulate

9. At the critical point within the nucleus of the atom, a point incidentally that is one hundred thousand times smaller than the whole atom, it is impossible to fully distinguish the dual aspect of the atomic entities that are fundamentally contradictory: 'Depending on how we look at them, they appear sometimes as particles, sometimes as waves; and this dual nature is also exhibited by light which can take the form of electromagnetic waves or of particles.' Fritjof Capra, *The Tao of Physics* (Boston: Shambhala, 1991), p67.

cellular organisms of microbiology if it leads us to the presumption of life spontaneously emerging from inorganic matter, a presumption that would be as miraculous as anything found in scripture.[10]

It is not enough to hold the forces of nuclear energy in one's hand like a spear, if we still resemble primitive beings and have not yet learned the awesome responsibility of such monumental forces of nature. It is not sufficient any longer to listen through rarefied instruments to the whispering of the galaxies any more than it is enough to see flickers of light through sophisticated space telescopes that provide definition and scope of the initial seconds of the Big Bang without realizing the revelatory insights that such a knowledge should convey. It is not enough to examine the great coil of DNA that has encoded the very alphabet and language of life if we deny life its very origin and source in the divine Creator.

In our contemporary search for knowledge, as we grapple with the reams of information coming from the distant galaxies in the universe and the swarming cells of our own bodies, we seem to be searching for a knowledge for its own sake without a view to the inner revelation that would substantiate all that we come to know about ourselves and the surrounding universe. The human being, both traditional and modern, is a searcher, that much is clear and as such, he exhibits the desire to know the unknown. Yet the question remains: Have we advanced from the stone age to the age of quantum mechanics only to rest content with an image of the human self as a physical organism without the transfiguring quality of the Spirit that is both Origin of all existence and Source of all reality?

The human psyche and soul has advanced from the stone age to the age of quantum mechanics because it is at heart searcher, a visionary and a listener, not of itself but of some transcendent being that extends far beyond this realm and of which the soul is but a pale reflection. Archaic visions of early souls still exist in the ruins of Stonehenge and in the primitive cave drawings in France. They

10. Richard Dawkins confesses that 'we may never know for certain,' but this does not stop him from extravagant speculation: 'The triggering event of a replication bomb is the spontaneous arising of self-replicating yet variable entities.' *River out of Eden* (London: Weidenfeld & Nicolson, 1995), p137.

have worshipped the Supreme Being throughout time and space by many names, just as the entire manifested creation worships the Divinity by being what it is in its essence and nothing more.

Let us turn away for a moment from the mesmerizing facts of modern science concerning galaxies and atoms and cells in order to look within, into the depths of the human imagination. We listen and see by virtue of abilities and faculties that we have had no part in creating; but if we dream, we dream of wonders and miracles of our own creation that no one can take away from us. If by chance we discover the source of a knowledge that is both universal and complete and adopt it as our own, then we will be fulfilling the aspirations of those primitive souls whose carved images in the dark caves of primitive time would prove to reflect, not a self-image of the human being as a material form, but an image of the Self as the ultimate source of all atoms, cells, and stars.

II

THE KNOWLEDGE
OF A TRUE BEGINNING

And in the earth are signs for those whose faith is sure.
And (also) in yourselves. Can you not see?
(60:20-21)

If all the trees were pens and all the seas were ink to record God's
speech, they would be exhausted before God's speech ran out
(18:109)

OUR SEARCH FOR THE AUTHENTIC SOURCES of knowledge leads us back through time to the moment of the initial creation when the universe virtually exploded into being from a single, compacted point or what the traditions call the primordial point. In our pursuit of an authentic knowledge of reality, we return once again to the source, at the moment of the initial creation of the universe, or what modern science curiously refers to as the 'Big Bang'. God's existence is eternal, but the knowledge of God's existence begins with the act of the initial creation, what modern science erroneously refers to as the 'initial singularity'. What science envisions as a singularity is actually the first manifestation of multiplicity, a multiplicity that will virtually characterize a created universe that reflects unity through multiplicity, the absolute through the relative, and the infinite through the finite. The secret of the divine mystery, which is the universal enigma that modern science aspires to uncover and categorize as a unified theory of knowledge, lies embedded within the very substance and manifestation of the creation as the One, the Absolute and the Infinite to the extent that the spiritual traditions refer to the universal creation as the supreme Body of God.

We have, of course, a serious disparity of opinion between the theory of cosmic origins portrayed through modern science and the perennial explanation of the creation set forth in the great scriptures of the world religions. In fact, the two predominant worldviews of the modern age are on parallel tracks that are moving in opposite directions. The Biblical *fiat lux* (let there be light) and the Quranic *kun fa yakoon* (be and it becomes) encapsulate within the divine speech of revelation the initial impulse of the Divinity to commence the unfolding of His Self Disclosure at the dawn of creation.

The *fiat lux* of the Bible emphasizes the visual image of light that is symbolic of a process that existentiated order from chaos,[1] while the Quranic *kun fa yakoon* refers to the auditory sound KUN that virtually initiated the divine act of creation. The scientific model of the universe leads us back to the horizon of time at the moment of initial singularity beyond which the theoretical model of the universe portrayed by modern science breaks down. Any further speculation concerning the nature of reality has no consequence because it lies outside the paradigm of science. The traditional model of the universe leads us beyond the celestial horizon to an atemporal moment whose real singularity lies in its access into the mega-realm of Supreme Unity. As such, the known universe is an observable reality within the context of a greater, unseen Reality that has created it and continues to sustain it.

In its search for the knowledge of universal origins, modern science takes us back to the edge of the time/space continuum at the outer periphery of the known universe, and then comes to an abrupt halt. Seemingly, it is enough to know that the universe began

---

1. The Hebrew word for morning is *boker* but its root implies that which is orderly or able to be discerned, remembering the primordial polarity of order and chaos, the order implicit in the light of morning as opposed to the chaos of darkness (*erev*). Moreover, according to the Islamic traditions, 'the first thing that God created was light.'

'in the beginning',[2] but the questions of *how* it began and more philosophically *why* find no place in the scientific inquiry, perhaps for no reason other than that the answer lies outside the parameters of its sources of knowledge, namely human reason and the physical senses, supported by the consistent and verifiable laws of nature, and is therefore irrelevant. Yet the 'how' and 'why' of the origin of the universe are questions that do not easily surrender their secret to human curiosity and linger at the gate of human inquiry challenging humanity to uncover the answer. The universal questions simply don't go away and continue to point to the ever enduring human presentiment that there is a purpose to the universe that belies the random chance of evolution, the spontaneous appearance of life, or the explosion of an unexpected universe in setting the ground for the laws of nature.

The origin of the universe[3] is an important question for people of today not only because it tells us something about the creation of the universe and the emergence of life, but perhaps more importantly, it tells us something about the true nature of the sources of knowledge that are made available to religion and science. According to Steven Hawking,[4] at the time of the big bang—if we can speak of such a thing as 'time' in that rarefied context of prelude and predawn—the density of the universe and the curvature of space-time

---

2. Not 'in the beginning of time', for example, as opposed to the atemporal context within the envelope of eternity. In fact, it is only within the last 30 years of this century that the modern scientific establishment has come around to the Biblical and Quranic view. From the time of Aristotle 2,300 years ago, scientific theory held the universe to be eternal. Now we accept the theory of the Big Bang as a 'popular wisdom'.

3. 'There is hidden under the conception of creation a more fundamental state of affairs which is in itself atemporal, namely God's being the ultimate source of all existent things. From this point of view, creation is nothing but a special form in which this essentially atemporal state of affairs is conceived and represented by the human mind in accordance with the rules of the "domain of reason". In other words, imagination cannot represent, the intellect cannot conceive of, God's being the ultimate ground of existence for everything except in the form of a temporal event, called "creation".' Toshihiko Izutsu, *Creation and the Timeless Order of Things* (Ashland, OR: White Cloud Press, 1994), pp130–131.

4. *A Brief History of Time*, p50.

would have been infinite. However, mathematics, which is the lodestone of modern science, does not really deal with infinite numbers, much less with the concept of infinity. As such, the general theory of relativity predicts that there is a point in the universe where the theory itself breaks down. This is what mathematicians call a 'singularity', a word that actually provides the layman with more meaning than intended, for what could be more singular than the explosion and expansion of the universe from a single, infinitely compacted and centered creative point.

From the point of view of having information drawn from some kind of ultimate 'source', the scientific theory of universal origins fails on fundamental levels, partly because there is no source knowledge to speak of, but rather a dead-end theory bereft of any nascent mystery, and partly because it simply does not make sense and is without reference to anything people can freely associate with either mentally or spiritually. As a scientific theory, it remains incomplete because it cannot tell us *how* the universe began and its power of prediction is fundamentally negative: it tells us that all physical theories break down at the beginning of the universe. Indeed, the origin of the universe according to modern science is a singularity precisely because the space-time continuum cannot be extended that far and continue to be what it is.

In fact, much speculation is made concerning the age of the universe[5] based on the assumption that if we can calculate how fast the universe is expanding, we can reverse that expansion back in time to the moment when the entire universe was contained within a single point. In fact, much of the calculation concerning the expanding universe is based on assumptions, such as the uniformity of the laws of nature in every time and place. To measure the rate of expansion, for example, we must measure the rate at which distant galaxies are moving away from our galaxy. Sounds feasible enough perhaps, but the reality of the situation is otherwise. In truth, we are able to measure relative distances through what is called the Cepheid brightness-to-distance calculation and this can be done out to nearly 100

5. The figure generally sited is 15 billion years old, although this number is usually housed within a range somewhere between 10 and 20 billions years.

million light years. The universe, however, extends to some 10 to 20 billion lights years. In other words, we are measuring less than 1 percent of the universe and assuming analogously that it represents the entire universe.[6]

According to the traditional perspective, it is by virtue of the spoken word 'in the beginning' that the question of the sources and true nature of knowledge is resolved. What, after all, does it mean to begin and how does it relate to the question of time whose frame of reference we cannot seem to transcend?[7] From the scientific point of view, it means none other than the commencement of a mystery that will never be resolved, a mystery that is self-professed and self-fulfilled within the framework of its own theories since 'beyond the beginning' lies outside the established framework of science. From the spiritual point of view, however, it means none other than the resolution of the perennial mystery that lies embedded within the very fabric of the universe and within the texture of the world of nature that is its natural expression. In believing that the phenomenal universe was eternal, traditional science over the millennia was able to avoid the major pitfall of a beginning in its worldview. The world as eternal rather than having a beginning permitted science until recently to avoid the question of a Beginner, or more appropriately, to use the Quranic terminology, an Originator (al-Mubdi), a Creator (al-Kha'liq), and a Being capable of expanding (al-Ba'sit) and sustaining (al-Muqît) the universe.

The universe, indeed the very existence of the cosmos, points beyond itself to a universal principle and first cause. When the Bible asserts the well-known phrase 'in the beginning', are we to interpret the Biblical in principio as an initiation and principle of time in a timely sense or a timely principle in a metaphysical sense that can serve as a reference point and framework within which to understand the genesis of the creation and the act of the Creator. In this

6. For more information on this point, see the recent publication of Gerald L. Schroeder, *The Science of God* (New York: Broadway Books, 1997), pp198–200.

7. Thomas Aquinas wrote centuries ago in his *Summa Contra Gentiles* (II, 35:15): 'God brought into being creation and time simultaneously.' In his *De Civita Dei* (11.6), he has also left us with this insight: 'Beyond all doubt, the world was not made *in* time, but *with* time.'

context, the knowledge of the true beginning finds its 'source' in God Himself who lies outside the reference point of time and outside the framework of the cosmos as such. Time actually begins in eternity through a vertical descent as a macrocosmic manifestation of a metacosmic Principle. Therefore, neither time nor its source-point in eternity are within the reach of modern science and cannot be fully categorized by its dispassionate and cold scrutiny.

Instead, the initial singularly presents itself, in the words of Wolfgang Smith,[8] as an 'incurably transcendent' point from which, according to modern scientific theory, the entire universe has sprung and continues to expand. This point is actually the origin of the Metacosmic Center that initiates the true Beginning when the universe was brought into existence. It is the result of the Creative Act whose point within the Center and whose time at the Beginning affirm the unity of the creation within the very fold of a Divine and Transcendent Being who, through an act of vertical causation that originates outside of time and space, actually creates the continuum in which the universe is made possible. In this way, the revealed sources of knowledge clarify the event—perhaps the non-event, for what can happen outside the framework of time—of the initial creation and re-create in the words of scripture the knowledge of the true Beginning.

❨ ❨ ❨

WITHIN THE COLD NIGHT and boundless realm of sempiternity, God initiated the first act of creation, not with a gesture but through the power of sound.[9] Out of the infinite silence beyond the

---

8. *Cosmos and Transcendence* (Peru, IL: Sherwood Sugden & Company, 1990), p110.

9. The use of sacred sound transcends individual spiritual traditions. There are Hindu cosmogonic myths that include the creation of the world from the primordial sound associated with the sacred mantra *Om*. According to Rabindranath Tagore in his *Sadhana*: '*Om* is the symbolic word for the infinite, the perfect, the eternal. The sound as such is already perfect and represents the wholeness of things. All our religious contemplations begin with *Om* and end with *Om*.'

celestial horizon, from the profound depths and absolute zenith representing the axial mystery of the Unknown, from the very origin, source and center of Cosmic Quintessence, The Supreme Being had spoken, thus initiating all that was to be, will be and is in the cosmic universe. Creative sound marks the genesis of a cosmic movement that had a 'beginning' and will continue to begin as an on-going creative event until the envelope of time ultimately closes down and merges back into the spectrum of eternity.

The revelation portrays divine sound as having initiated the manifestation, rhythm, and harmony of the universe. Therefore, it is not as farfetched as it may first seem to the modern mentality that, through sound, humanity will once again find the possibility of fine-tuning themselves with the spiritual vibrations that are in the very nature of things and strike the holy cord that is in the original nature (*al-fitrah*) of the human being. Both ancient and more modern scriptures suggest that the creative act in its first step towards manifestation was audible, followed by the visible, and ultimately the tangible signs of the universe.

The absolute use of sound makes its first appearance at the time of cosmic genesis, when the Divinity desired to be made manifest, remembering the traditional saying in Islam that reports God saying in a *hadith qudsi*: 'I was a hidden treasure and wanted to be known. Therefore I created the universe.' In order to re-create what happened at the source of knowledge and in the beginning of time, we need to return for a moment to the prelude and dawn of the primordial wilderness and listen! The inaudible was made audible, the invisible was made visible, and the intangible was made tangible.

The Quranic revelation echoes the mythological substance of many of the great traditions when it says that the noble creation and the subsequent unfolding of the entire universe commenced in the beginning, *in illo tempore*, with the sound of a Divine Command made manifest in the Islamic tradition through the Arabic word *kun*, *Be*, followed by the revealed Arabic *fa yakoun*, 'and lo it becomes'! With these words, nothing was negated by becoming something (*creatio ex nihilo*) with the utterance of the sound/word KUN (BE). All of creation, including the very act of creation, can be reduced to the sacred sound of a primordial utterance, a cosmic

sound that was to translate the creative act into the full manifestation of the universe. Cosmic energy was activated and all existent
things could be and were actualized within a time-space continuum, subject to the Command (*al-amr*) of God. The stuff of the
universe began with the instantaneous crystallization[10] of the existential energy of the universe that has been created by the Divine
Being. 'To Him is due the primal origin of the heavens and the
earth. When He decreeth a matter, He said to it: 'Be!' And it is' (2:
117). In this way, revelation recreates with precision what took
place at the beginning of time, at the moment beyond the threshold of which modern science confesses it can say nothing because
the matrices within which it operates did not exist. All of creation,
including the very act of creation, can be reduced to the sacred
sound of a primordial word, a cosmic sound that set in motion the
creative act that became the universe.

Thus, the Quranic scripture depicts the great moment when the
cosmic genesis, in the form of a potential or budding universe,
what modern scientists call the Big Bang, came into being with the
word KUN. The actualization of a formal universe immediately led
(*fa yakoun*) to the emergence of a *knowledge* and this *knowledge*
ultimately expressed itself as an *action*. The triad existence–
knowledge–action began with a reverberation of sound that
became a word that has echoed down through the eons of time
and will continue to do so until the Day of Judgment when the
universe will *fold up* like a scroll, according to the symbolic eschatology of the Quran, with yet another sound, that of a *Tremendous
Blast* and a *Great Cry*. According to revealed scripture, the concor-
dance of energy and sound both initiated and will terminate the
existence of the cosmic universe.

The mystery of sound and the evolution of speech embody more
than mere language and words. Behind the mystery of sound lies
the principle of all mental representations and communication.
Whether it is in the form of audible, visible, or thought symbols, the
use of sound, symbolic language and the written word is able to

---

10. 'And Our Command is but a single (act), like the twinkling of an eye' (54:
50).

convey a knowledge of thoughts and dreams, of aspirations and sentiments, of culture and art, of science and religion, until the arrival of revelation which conveys the highest knowledge made available to humanity through the use of vibratory sound, namely the essential and redeeming knowledge of God. In fact, revelatory sound has the compelling, mystical power to call up the direct perception of reality through intelligible thought and sacred vision when the divine revelation descends from God to man.

Sound and word continued to play a vital role in the unfolding of the cosmic drama. The great, human, narrative epic of the unfolding of the universal soul originated with the bold affirmation of the human soul and its hallowed '*Yes!*' In the pre-dawn of the creation, the Spirit of God asked the primordial soul the cosmic question: 'Am I not your Lord' (*Alastu bi rabbikum*)? The soul answered willingly: 'Yes, we witness You!' (*Balaa, shahidna* [7:172]) The very nature of the divine question presupposes the element of choice, a cosmic question answered by the human soul in response. The soul was given the choice to establish a sacred trust between the human and the Divine, a trust most notably that was offered to other aspects of Nature, according to the Quranic verse 33:72 that states: 'We did, indeed, offer the Trust to the heavens and the earth and the mountains, but they refused to undertake it, being afraid thereof: But the human soul undertook it'. He could also have been afraid and refused presumably, as did the mountains, the heavens and the earth. Instead, at the dawn of creation, man's first act of worship was to accept the responsibility of a covenant with God, a sacred trust whose implicit blessing was knowledge of self in complement to the knowledge of God. Through consciousness of self and knowledge of God, and through a free will that was activated by this momentous choice, the human soul became a spiritual being ready to fulfill the mandate of the human condition that was embodied and enshrined within the context of a sacred trust with the Divinity.

Through revelation, the importance of sound and speech has been made known and its significance plays a vital role at both the beginning and the end of time. God spoke, thus formally initiating the act of creation for all time. The soul then affirmed the sacred trust with its noble, human affirmation. As primordial man, Adam

walked and spoke with God, meaning that he had a direct perception of the Divinity, without any barrier or veil. He was given the
names of things, thus identifying all aspects of the creation with an
individual and unique name that empowered it with substantive
meaning. The Word in the form of sacred, revelatory speech came
to future generations as the ultimate source of knowledge in lieu of
Adam's forgetting for one vital moment in time the very source of
his being. Finally, as a prelude to the coming of the Day of Judgment, the end of time will be heralded with the sound of a blast and
a cry.

Humans also speak to God through prayer, thus formally initiating the return to their Origin and Source. We worship and pray, and
through prayer, we can articulate the heartfelt sentiments of our
innermost being. Through words, we identify ourselves; through
words, we worship the Divinity; through words, we recreate our
being with the very Origin and Source of all that exists in the creation. Through words, we can articulate a consciousness of God
that can be listened to as well as heard.

❨   ❨   ❨

TO SPEAK OF THE AUTHENTICITY of knowledge is to refer to its
sources and wellsprings. The echo that comes down from the
Source represents the auditory and visual residue of the universal
and primordial knowledge common to humanity that has emerged
within time to become the expression of a universal world reality.
No pragmatic or scientific knowledge can explain the mysterious
existence of a snow crystal, and yet there is knowledge imbedded
within its design and beauty that raises the question of origins.
Similarly, every living thing exhibits its own poignant sound and its
own characteristic voice and remembers the mystery of sound at
the initial creation that brought the universe into being. The melan-
choly cry of the peacock, the busy chirping of sparrows and the
emotive song of the nightingale remember and reflect through
sound a unique and individual soul that remembers the abiding
Spirit that conveys to all life its vitality and living quality.

To speak of mystery is to speak of the miracle of Nature. We can summon the image of a star and trace its pale light back to the shaft of light emanating from a distant galaxy, a beam of light that has travelled down through the darkness of outer space to meet the physical receptacle of my admiring eye where it is translated into a consciousness of other worlds beyond the horizon of our knowledge and experience. 'The earth is full of signs evidencing the work of Allah and also within your own selves. Will ye not then see?' (51: 20). Everything, whether it be a plant, an animal or a cosmic shaft of light was understood by traditional peoples as signs of a higher reality and expressions of a divine cosmology. 'Traditional metaphysics sees the universe not as a multitude of facts or opaque objects each possessing an independent reality of their own, but as myriads of symbols reflecting higher realities.'[11] Phenomena appear as fact, but become transparent to realities that transcend them. The phenomena of nature were symbols that linked the visible with the invisible and with sacred sounds that echo from Heaven to earth.

Three fundamental questions concerning the true knowledge of reality have proven since time immemorial to be as enigmatic and mysterious as they are magnetic and challenging to the human mentality. They are: What is the universe? What is life? What is human nature? The search for the answers to these three questions represents the unending search of humanity for the universal principle that all knowledge and experience can be referred to. The answers to these questions would finally solve for humanity the perennial mystery of the universe, of life and of the soul. Perhaps that is why we have no definitive answers to these questions except what comes to us through the self-disclosure of the Divinity through Revelation, through Nature and through the human being.

The answers to these questions have perennially eluded humanity because knowledge of the reality, which is the goal of the search for the essential knowledge, is a difficult concept for the human mind to grasp. One reason for this is the fact that the gap between the physical world and the experiential world is wide and disconnected.

11. S.H. Nasr, *Religion and the Order of Nature* (Oxford: Oxford University Press, 1996), p15.

We see the physical world but we do not see the world of experience. If we proclaim reality to be based in the phenomenal world of matter, then what are we to make of the non-corporal world of light and sound and color, not to mention the wealth of human thought, emotion and experience that is beyond the scrutiny of science but that exists as a conscious event and a truly felt experience.

Another reason why coming to terms with the knowledge of reality eludes the grasp of humanity is that, according to Islamic doctrine, the idea of Reality is an alternative name of God. Therefore, to know the reality would be to know God and we can see and know God only indirectly, from behind a veil or 'through a glass darkly'. That is why we come to know God through His revelatory self-disclosures, namely through revelation, through the universe, through nature, through the diverse manifestation of life throughout the natural world, and finally through people, who by coming to know themselves will come to know the Divinity.

Furthermore, another reason why the true nature of the reality remains a mystery to us lies in the fact that reality doesn't begin, become or end in the same way that we understand phenomena to commence and take place within the span of time. Reality is a now and forever eternal event, and does not take part as such in the continuum of time and space as we experience it. As the pinnacle of ultimate knowledge, it is beyond the envelope of the universe; or for want of a better phrase, the true reality envelops the universe within its own spectrum and field. How, then, can we come to 'know' it? Moreover, having said that reality exists and always is, we as human beings are forever surprised to realize that reality is a truth as well as an action, an objective truth no less, as well as a dynamic happening. Fourthly, to be real for humanity, reality must be experiential and thus should be experienced in all its truth. This, then, is the crux of the problem: What is truth and, in consequence, what is truth's reality?

These questions need to be posed at the outset of this work and have a right to be asked because the reality to which we refer (and its attendant truth) is implicitly not the same as the reality that is portrayed through the modern scientific worldview. This in turn causes a kind of split inference in the mindset and mentality of people today who think one way about their deepest urges based on the proclamations of modern science as ultimate fact, but feel another, deeper and unsubstantiated longing for something greater that lies beyond the known facts. What is needed is a reality and a truth that is universal. What is needed is a professed reality that expresses objectively established truths and is an intelligible expression of a dynamic and living world-feeling that embraces everyone and permits humanity to experience the meaning of transcendence in this world as a truth that is both real and truly felt. Reality need not be conceptualized as an ill-defined expression of 'beyond' that represents a different sphere from our world, or an elusive, paradisal world in some other realm that is disassociated from what we experience here and now, as it is often portrayed in the religions; nor is it a purely physical and phenomenal reality of the senses as is portrayed by modern science. On the contrary, it is a reality that underlies daily existence with its overwhelming presence, its absolute objectivity and its eternal truth, a reality reflected within as an enlightened consciousness, a perceptive subjectivity, and a wisdom that is experienced and truly felt.

Perhaps our most prominent characteristic lies in the duality of our beings. As worldly beings, we turn outward to experience the multiplicity of the sensory world, but as spiritual beings, we look within, to the wholeness of our center and the timelessness of our origin, in order to become conscious of the metaphysical unity that underlies the multiplicity of the physical universe. In searching either for a unified theory of knowledge according to modern science and the essential knowledge of the One according to the traditions, we end up merely counting the multiple. On the contrary, it is through the experience of multiplicity that we can come to know of the singularity of its source. According to certain traditions, all of mathematics exists because of the multiple possibilities of the number one.

(((

IF THE DIVINITY IS THE PRIMAL ORIGIN and Original Source of all knowledge as embodied in the revelation, in nature and in humanity, then the revelation as a transcendent world, cosmic nature as a book of phenomenal existence and the human as microcosm and world within a world represent the intermediary sources of knowledge in the form of a written book, as a theatre of nature reflecting through multiple mirrors the Face of the Beloved ('Wherever you turn, there is the Face of God' [2:115]), and as the human revelation in which the human person becomes a living theophany of the Reality. The correspondence between *insan* (the human entity), the cosmos and revelation is crucial in the religious configuration of Islam, partly because each element forms a contiguous part as the source material for the religion and partly because the written wisdom, the natural wisdom and the human wisdom contained in the scripture, nature and the human being all deliver the essential knowledge that bespeaks of the true nature of the one Reality.

As such, revelation, nature and the human soul each exhibit signs that are direct reflections of the Divinity and these 'signs' are intended to serve humanity as a means of lifting the veil that separates humanity from direct knowledge of the Divinity. The revealed words of the Quran descend from the Mind of Allah, pass through the mind and were delivered orally by the Messenger of Islam and ultimately set down as a written book (*al-Qur'an al-Tadwini*) with verses that in Arabic are called *ayat* which when translated means 'signs' or 'verses', linking the verses of the Book with the well known Quranic verse 'We will show them Our signs on the horizon and within themselves' (41:53). The cosmos itself, referred to in Arabic as the cosmic Quran (*al-Qur'an al-Takwini*) or the book of existence,[12] represents a vast book in complement to the Islamic book of revelation, and like the revealed scripture, it also contains signs and symbols that have the power to reveal as much as they conceal and

12. The 8th/14th-century Sufi 'Aziz al-Din Nasafi has written the following concerning the book of nature: 'Each day destiny and the passage of time set this book before you, *sura* for *sura*, verse for verse, letter for letter, and read it to you ... like one who sets a real book before you and reads it to you line for line, letter for letter, that you may learn the content of these lines and their letters.' Quoted in *Islamic Spirituality: Foundations*, ed., Seyyed Hossein Nasr (New York: Crossroad, 1987), p355.

possess levels of meaning that can serve the needs of every mentality and that ultimately lead toward a complete understanding of the true nature of reality. Finally, the human being is a book of self-revelation whose story becomes a conscious human life and whose thoughts and actions become the signs and symbols of a tale well lived.

Therefore, the *ayat* manifest themselves within the Holy Book, within the macrocosmic universe, and within the human soul, or in the words of the Quran 'on the distant horizon and within their own selves.' 'The Quran and the great phenomena of nature are twin manifestations of the divine act of Self-revelation. For Islam, the natural world in its totality is a vast fabric into which the "signs" of the Creator are woven.'[13] Humans can understand themselves as a sign of God, the cosmos as a grand theophany and mirror of the Divine Qualities and Attributes, and the revealed book that contains all the verses and thus all the knowledge they need to know in order to come to terms with themselves and the universe as the *vestigia Dei*, according to Christian terminology. Each element has its own form of metaphysics and its own mode of prayer, humans through living the sacred narrative of their lives, the cosmos through being the sanctuary and theatre wherein the Divinity can become manifest, and revelation by recreating for humanity aspects of the mind of God through words and phrases.

We have concentrated our thoughts in this chapter, not on the fact of the creation and its genesis as you might expect to find within the modern scientific framework, but on its truth as a source and well-spring of knowledge. It is not enough to know that the universe has begun any more than it is enough to know that every single soul has begun. Neither the cosmos nor the human being can be exhausted in their implications by their physical aspects alone. Both take part in a reality that extends far beyond the limitations of the physical world that in and of itself is merely a three-dimensional and limited aspect of reality.

13. Charles Le Gai Eaton, *Islam and the Destiny of Man* (Albany, NY: SUNY Press, 1985), p 87.

According to modern science, the universe constitutes a single manifestation of reality, one level as it were, while all speculation concerning intangible, spiritual or in any sense otherworldly phenomena is dismissed as an expression of 'unreality'. The objective of modern science is to uncover a unified theory of everything that would bring all the known laws of nature into a single comprehensive framework. According to the traditional perspective, however, the universe partakes of levels of reality. The message of its very magnitude and breadth amply attests to that truth. Its billions and billions of galaxies swirling around a central core and its light-years upon light years, reflecting as they do both immense distance and time, would only numb the mind with their unreal and incomprehensible magnitude without the enlightening perspective of the Transcendent Center that unifies both the human being and the universe into a single principle of knowledge at source. As such, in addition to the Quran, the universe itself is a great book of knowledge that can teach us far more about ourselves and our world than we might have thought possible or imaginable.

To understand the vision of the human world and the world of nature as being irrevocably related to the world of revelation is to live and experience ourselves and the world we live in as the sacred and concomitant realities that they are. Without a sense of the sacred and without a feeling for the sublime articulation of the Whole, we would simply remain the three-dimensional figurines we now envision ourselves to be, on the road to self-destruction and ultimately oblivion. We need to abandon a paradigm of thought that relies solely on facts and figures to determine our self-image and worldview. We need to see for what it really is the one-sided and narrow perspective of modern science whose vision does not extend beyond the perception of self and that uses human reason alone to interact with the stuff of matter that constitutes the physical world.

When we think of the universe, how do we picture it and therefore what does it mean to us? Do we recreate in our mind's eye, for example, the dark matter and black holes, the red-hot suns and white dwarfs, the vast distances that preclude any thought of deep space travel and the tremendous aeons of time required to allow the universe to happen? Or do we recreate in our mind's eye the vision of a sublime totality that lives eternally as a Transcendent Center; but that has created the primordial point that expanded into the grand manifestation of a living and organic universe, because this transcendent and eternal Center wanted 'to be known' and therefore executed the miracle of cosmic and human consciousness? Do the laws that govern what we witness to be an ordered cosmos exist as the expression of an inevitable virtuality and a blind expression of random fact, or are they the evidence of a divine self-disclosure and the reflection of an intelligence, the Supreme Intelligence if you will, that has created, governs and sustains the universe? When the spiritual traditions say that the human is the microcosm and the universe is the macrocosm, implying that the universe exists within the human just as the human exists within the universe, what does that mean and does anyone really know? Whatever may be the true answer, one thing is clear: In whatever sense the universe is truly reflected within each person, can I claim to be that person? Are the order, design and purpose reflected within nature a motivating force in my awareness? Finally, is the universe a conscious and living reality, just as I know myself to be and am?

We began this chapter by relying on the source material of a *hadith qudsi*, a Holy Tradition in the words of the Divinity, that suggests the ultimate rationale for the creation of both humanity and the universe. The modern psyche has a concept of the universe that is staggering in its proportions, benumbing the mind with its vast time frames and incredible distances because it is outside of us and we are not apart of it in some qualitative manner. The ancient and traditional scale of the universe is equally awesome, but in an entirely different way. The modern scale of the universe exceeds all of our expectations of quantity by dwarfing us in size in relation to the vast physical perspective and leaving us bereft of a purpose and a meaning that can integrate us into the Whole, thereby disassociating modern individuals from the world of nature and the universe in which they inevitably takes part. In addition, the modern speculative discoveries of such things are dark matter, black holes and parallel universes have no symbolic value. Their theoretical existence may intrigue the mind with its technical virtuosity and its imaginative flare, but in terms of how they might possibly relate to humanity and the world, they mean nothing.

Once upon a time and forever more, the sources of traditional knowledge will continue to inspire the minds and hearts of believers everywhere. The night sky will always be the 'city of God' and the vast cosmic universe will always be a magnificent universal book (*ayat*//verses) and a mirror reflection of the Divinity. The traditional scale of the universe fully establishes the value of the qualitative experience behind the cold face of quantity. It weaves an intricate web of purpose and a hierarchy of meaning that permits people to find their place in the universe precisely because the essential elements of the universe exist within the mind, heart and soul, namely knowledge, intelligence, existence, life, and consciousness. The mystery of cosmic genesis and the knowledge of a true beginning lie hidden within the mystery of a transcendent consciousness that has proclaimed as an eternal remembrance: 'I was a hidden treasure and wanted to be known. Therefore, I created the world.'

III

THE MYSTIC PEN
AND THE GUARDED TABLET

*Say: The (Quran) was sent down by Him Who knows the mystery in
the heavens and the earth; He is Oft-Forgiving, Most Merciful.*
(25:6)

*Recite! And thy Lord is Most Bountiful. He Who taught through the
use of the pen; taught man what he knew not.*
(96:3–5)

PERHAPS NOTHING CHALLENGES the sedentary, rationalist and
earth-bound mindset of the modern psyche more than the traditional concept of revelation. That the eternal word of a Divinity
could cut through the fabric of the space-time continuum of this
world with the knife blade of a knowledge of the ultimate reality
seems incredible to the modern mind fully steeped in the believabil-
ity of matter and totally dependent upon the power of human reason to lead the way through the dark mystery and paradox of life.
To believe in a universal Logos, representing the mind of God
through a divine discourse that can shatter the illusion of our world
by its very entrance into the world of multiplicity and then re-con-
stitute and unify the pieces back into a single and unified tapestry of
truth, requires an openness of mind and a willingness to seek
knowledge anywhere that the modern, scientific mentality is unwilling to entertain.

The reality of a descent of knowledge in the form of revelation
simply will not go away, however, in spite of the skeptical denial of

modern scientists and contemporary sophisticates the world over, who reject outright all higher forms of spiritual experience and other levels of reality by insisting upon the doctrine of matter over mind and reason over intellection in the pursuit of a knowledge of the true reality. Revelation continues to remain the key to the perennial mysteries[1] of creation, life-genesis, and human origins precisely because the revealed word of the Divinity serves humanity viscerally, intellectually, emotionally and spiritually as the principal source of knowledge of primordial origins, because it traces the origin of the creation and the genesis of life forms back to the Divine Being and because it identifies once and for all the true nature of Reality within the framework of the First Cause and Ultimate Source of all creation.

What haunts the worldview portrayed by the modern scientific establishment is the fact that human reason, together with the provability of matter as the basis of the scientific method and the cornerstone of the worldview shaped by the findings of science, is not a true, archetypal source of knowledge. Rather it is an instrument, indeed a key human faculty, for dealing with the demands of all primary knowledge. In and of itself reason has no substance; it will not tell you anything that it has not already been fed from elsewhere, through revelation, through intuition, through the thinking process, and even, perhaps especially, through the senses. Yet reason and the provability of matter constitute the basic sources of knowledge and the norm for establishing the objectivity within the scientific framework, giving birth to the secular philosophy of rationalism as the polar opposite—and the modern-day answer—to revelation. Rationalism continues to retain a deep-seated conviction in the physical senses as the definitive means of providing information that is certain and unquestionable, thus attesting to the objectivity of matter, a conviction that persists in the popular imagination in spite of the fact that quantum mechanics has virtually demolished the concept of solid matter as a valid working hypothesis. According to Frithjof

---

1. 'Whether we like it or not, we live surrounded by mysteries, which logically and existentially lead us towards transcendence.' Frithjof Schuon, *From the Divine to the Human* (Bloomington, IN: World Wisdom Books, 1981), p141.

Schuon: 'Scientists condemn themselves to seeing only what they believe; logic for them is their desire not to see what they do not want to believe.'[2] Seeing is believing; but more importantly, not seeing is active disbelieving.

Schuon has aptly characterized the anti-spiritual ambiance of our time with the following words: 'One of the greatest successes of the devil was to create situations in which God and immortality appear unbelievable.'[3] During our modern era, if there is anything more difficult for the secular and scientific mind to accept as a working hypothesis and believe in than the idea of God, it is undoubtedly the traditional belief that revelation represents the absolute word of God, a belief still adhered to by over a billion Muslims across the globe who revere the sacred text by considering the book a universe in which they place the world of their lives. If a particular mentality refuses to believe in the idea of God, much less God Himself, then the concept of God 'speaking' to humanity through the words of a revealed communication will equally fall into the realm of a fantasy that modern sophisticates love to foster.

Similarly, if a person believes in God as a matter of spiritual instinct if not as a result of proven scientific observation such as the existence of matter,[4] simple logic demands that the Divinity convey the essential knowledge of the reality to humanity in some comprehensible manner. What better way for people to come to know in advance and eternally the essential knowledge they need to know in order to fulfill their human vocation and perfect themselves than through the Voice, the Word, indeed the very Mind and Consciousness of God, amounting to the ultimate act of benevolence and mercy[5] from the Divine to the human being. For millennia within many traditional cultures[6], sacred scripture has bridged the chasm

2. Ibid.

3. Ibid., p148.

4. Or does it? Physicists will now tell you otherwise in keeping with the indeterminate theory. The question of what is 'real' and what is 'illusory' is as controversial today as it has ever been through history, physics notwithstanding.

5. In the Islamic perspective, Allah is above all a benevolent Deity. Inscribed on the Throne (al-arsh) of God are the words: 'My Mercy precedes My Wrath.'

6. According to the Quran: 'Every nation has been sent a messenger' (10:47), thus attesting to both the universality and the particularity of revealed scripture for

that exists between the knowledge of the Divine and the ignorance of the human and will continue to do so, as long as there are people who can recognize the truth when they are confronted by its open and clear face.[7]

Part of the contemporary prejudice that exists against the possibility of the descent of a divine discourse from the Divine to the human lies in the fact that the modern mentality, in its surface approach to the mysteries of life and because of its literalist and form-based bias in its search for a knowledge of origins and final ends, makes a certain amount of simplistic assumptions about the real implications of a divine descent of knowledge without contemplating the full range, significance, and implications of such a happening. Many people today reject the concept of revelation, not through the logic of an intellectual argument and not through any mode of experimentation that examines the experience of billions of people over thousands of years. They reject it simply because it doesn't conform to their belief in the provability and thus the objectivity of matter and the supremacy of the human mind to reason its way through the labyrinthine mysteries of life based on the laws of mathematics and the rational experience of the senses. Modern science sets out to discover, study and catalogue the vast and infinite complexity of the Real on its own, without the aid of the first science of the traditional world, namely metaphysics. It relies on the world of physics rather than metaphysics and it pursues the science of the relative rather than knowledge of the Absolute. Indeed, it is partly because revelation identifies itself as the absolute word of God that modern science rejects it outright. According to the modern scientific worldview, human reason, inanimate matter and the physical senses establish the norm, set the standard and constitute the primary sources of knowledge concerning the true nature of reality.

There remains, however, a major existential conditional. What if, and admittedly it is a powerful conditional, the principal mysteries

every time and place, in addition to highlighting the importance placed on revelation as a divine communication.

7. "Wherever you turn, there is the Face of God' (2:115).

confronting humanity were never to be disclosed? What if, for example, there were no hope of ever realizing, through the strictly scientific process of inquiry, the essential knowledge that lies behind the face of the great and universal enigmas that season our lives with their unrelenting inscrutability and their unnerving power of attraction to extend the boundaries of human curiosity. After all, traditional history has amply proven that the Divinity has no special desire to reveal all and everything, and even the revelation itself is articulated in such a way that it is a key for the open-hearted and a veil to the hard-hearted, summarily protecting itself from disbelieving minds with a subtle air of impenetrability. The Divine Reality does not limit itself to revealing the multiple aspects of its Being. On the contrary, it conceals as much as it reveals, the ample proof of this being that God continues to conceal the knowledge of origins and final ends totally from strictly rational and secularist minds precisely because the revelation is as much a veil as it is a key. Perhaps that is why traditional peoples have always answered the existential question with their human affirmation of faith; perhaps that is why the modern, scientific community continues to answer the great metaphysical questions with their human denial of their truth.

〈　〈　〈

Without a doubt he saw him in the clear horizon. Neither doth he withhold grudgingly a knowledge of the Unseen.
(81:23, 24)

IN OUR INQUIRY into the sources of knowledge and the means through which humans can experience, realize and internalize the knowledge of the reality, we now turn to the earliest sources within the Islamic tradition in order to examine the extraordinary circumstances in which the Quran made its descent into the world, a vertical descent that cut through the fabric of 'this world' with the cutting edge knowledge of a transcendent reality, illuminating the dark mind of humanity with a flash of lightning. This miraculous occurrence pierced forever the world of appearances and left behind a religion and a way of life, the Islamic *din*, that made possible a new world of spiritual experience as a mercifully resolving overlay to the contingencies of this world.

In the religion of Islam, the Quran forms the absolute basis of the religion, including its knowledge, its doctrine, its spiritual practices, its rich symbolism, its sacred sentiments and its holy ambiance. When the verses of the Quran began to descend from the Divine Mind into the human receptacle of the Messenger Mohammed, upon whom blessings and peace, the religion itself began to manifest and take form since the religion is first and foremost the Quran from the point of view of source. When the verses came to completion, the Prophet died soon thereafter and the religion was considered completed and perfected.[8]

A brief glimpse at what occurred in Central Arabia during the 7th century AD, at a time when Europe was still in the Dark Ages, will highlight certain events and may reveal to the modern mentality an unexpected insight. The Holy Quran and the Traditions, commonly referred to in English with the Arabic word *hadith*, recall the miraculous event that occurred when the Archangel Gabriel first appeared to a simple Arab trader from Makkah with the initial verses of what were to become the full revelation of a Divine Being who identified Himself with the Supreme Name of Allah. At the time, this future Messenger of Islam was unsuspecting of the great role that was being placed upon his shoulders and was unacquainted as such with the full significance of both revelation and faith. 'And thus have We, by our command, sent inspiration to thee: Thou knewest not (before) what was Revelation and what was Faith, but We have made the (Quran) a Light, wherewith We guide such of our servants as We will; and indeed thou dost guide (mankind) to the straight path' (42:52).

---

8. 'This day have I perfected your religion for you, completed My favor upon you, and have chosen for you Islam as your religion' (5:3). This is the last verse revealed chronologically marking the termination of the Prophet's ministry in his earthly life.

Early biographical sources have recorded that the Prophet was about thirty-five years old, approximately five years before the first descent of the initial verses of the Quranic revelation, when he began to retire into a cave near Makkah, called the Hira cave, located within the *Jabal an-Nur*, the Mountain of Light. Traditionally, the cave[9] has been considered sacred space down through the ages, and thus was the perfect environment for the inward practices of contemplation and inner inquiry for a contemplative mind such that the Prophet had. People have been fascinated with caves for millennia and mystics and saints have traditionally retired to the isolation and safety of a natural cave because they offered perfect seclusion and were often inaccessible to both men and animals. The Prophet was merely following the example of earlier descendants of Ishmael who would periodically make retreats in mountain caves for the purposes of purification and enlightenment. The early sources[10] of the life of the Prophet record that he spoke of 'true visions' during these moments of retreat, visions that came to him clearly while he was at rest or asleep in the cave of Hira, visions that were 'like the breaking of the light of dawn.'

During the last days of the holy month of Ramadan[11], which was the traditional month of retreat even in pre-Islamic times, the Prophet saw something strange and unexpected in a seemingly miraculous dream during his sleep, a dream that ranged far beyond anything he had ever experienced before in his life. At first, he did not know what was happening to him, the shock of the experience was so raw and powerful. A Quranic verse has later documented

9. The Prophet was later to rely once again on a cave to escape with his companion Abu Bakr and hide from the pursuing Makkans during the *hegira* or flight to Medina, well-known in the Traditions because of the spider that sealed the cave with his web in order to deceive the Makkans into thinking that no one had entered the enclosure.

10. The following references to early sources and sayings of the Holy Prophet are taken from Martin Lings' well-known and respected book *Mohammed: His Life Based on the Earliest Sources* (Kuala Lumpur, Malaysia: Noordeen, 1988).

11. According to the Traditions, the Quran began to descend on a night identified as the *Laylat al-Qadr*, the Night of Measure and Power, a night that is 'better than a thousand months' (97:3).

and fully confirmed what occurred to the messenger at that time and why: 'He was taught by one mighty in power, endued with wisdom, for he appeared (in stately form) while he was in the highest part of the horizon, then he approached and came closer and was at a distance of but two bow-lengths or (even) nearer. So did (Allah) convey the inspiration to His Servant what He (meant) to convey' (53:5–10). Of course, the Divine Being does not speak directly to human beings. Rather God communicates with His human creation through intuition, through an angelic intermediary or from behind a veil. Moses heard the voice of God from behind the veil of a burning bush, while the Messenger of Islam saw and heard the celestial Messenger, the archangel Gabriel. 'It is not fitting for a man that God should speak to him except by inspiration, or from behind a veil, or by the sending of a Messenger to reveal, by God's permission, what God wills; for He is the Highest, Most Wise' (42:51).

The abrupt and unexpected visitant that he beheld was none other than an archangel in the form of a man. He was carrying what appeared to be a written document, enveloped in a precious piece of silk. The angel said: 'I am Gabriel. God has sent me to communicate to you His message.' He then intoned: 'Recite (or read) this' and the Prophet immediately replied: 'I am not a reciter (I do not know how to read).' In fact, the Prophet was *ummi*, meaning unlettered and unable to read; he was the pure, unstained vessel and thus the perfect receptacle to receive the divine revelation. Three times the Archangel exhorted him to 'Recite' and three times the Prophet replied that he was not able to read. Finally, the first revelation passed through his mind and out into the world: 'Recite (*iqra*') in the name of thy Lord who created, created man from a clot of blood. Read and thy lord is most bountiful, who has taught by the Pen, taught man what he knew not' (96:1–5).

Mohammed awoke, terrified by what he had experienced. Was this a devil? A spell? An otherworldly inspiration? A divine revelation? The simple Makkan merchant did not know exactly who and what he had encountered. Yet the words he had heard rang out like a bell and later he was to say: 'It was as though the words were written on my heart.' He fled the cave and proceeded down the side of the mountain, in a state of confusion and doubt. However, as he stumbled down the slope, he heard a voice saying 'O, Mohammed, thou art the Messenger of God and I am Gabriel!' The earliest sources record that he raised his eyes and saw the vision of Gabriel now as an angel, an image that filled the breadth of the horizon. 'Without a doubt he saw him in the clear horizon, neither doth he withhold grudgingly a knowledge of the Unseen' (81:23, 24). Again, the angel said: 'O Mohammed, thou are the Messenger of God and I am Gabriel!' Mohammed turned to descend the slope once again. Wherever he turned, however, whether to the north, south, east or west, he saw the magnificent archangel standing astride *the highest part of the horizon*. Finally, the angel turned away and the Prophet of Islam descended the slope and went to his house where his wife Khadijah comforted him, and consoled him by saying: 'You have always been generous, charitable and obliging to everyone poor and needy; God would certainly not abandon you, nor let you succumb to the devil.'[12]

It was a brief and stunning moment for the unsuspecting merchant from Makkah when the unseen had suddenly become visible and when the sacred Words of God had become audible. The Prophet had experienced an instance in which he was able to witness the monumental unveiling of one of the unseen mysteries (*al-ghayb*) that perennially protects, as from behind a veil, all direct knowledge of the Divinity. However, this was no ordinary human being; he was the messenger of God, the bearer of good news, and a warner, even if he is also identified in the Quran as 'a man from among yourselves'. Indeed, at that moment, in the deserts of western Arabia, the unseen mystery had commenced to become a living knowledge for all of humanity, both at that time and for future generations until the end of time as we know it.

The descent of the first verses of the Quranic revelation through an angelic messenger marked the formal descent of a divine knowledge to be preserved and acted upon by all the faithful within the earthly environment. As Divine Speech, it was an absolute and

12. Mohammed Hamidullah, *Mohammed Rasulullah* (Hyderabad: Deccan, 1974), p20.

final[13] communication of the Divine Being with the human being. After an initial interlude of silence that lasted for three years, the descent of the verses of the revelation continued to pass through the mind of the Messenger and out into the world of future generations for twenty-three years until just before the end of the Prophet's life.

What happened on that blessed night of initial descent marked the commencement of the revelation of the Word and the Book, the Holy Quran, which is *on a tablet well preserved* in the Paradise, a communication that represents the absolute Speech of the Divinity.[14] Once again, the Quranic verse bears repeating that we quoted earlier, which stated that humanity, will be shown signs (*ayat*), *on the horizon and within their own souls*. During the moments of revelation, the Prophet had become a kind of human horizon over which the miraculous and blessed communication from the Divinity continued to emerge until it had fully arrived within the human frame of reference and was completed. Through the import of the sacred words, all duality within the earthly sphere re-united once again in principle to become one in truth and in reality.

All Muslims love with a profound inner emotion their Prophet. The Messenger witnessed the initial descent of the Quranic revelation through the archangel Gabriel, a luminous and virtually invisible 'being' made momentarily visible to the human eye. He heard the first sacred sound, the first Word and the first verse that would come to be known the world over as the sacred speech of Allah. Throughout the course of his ministry, the verses of the Quran came to him, infiltrated his mind, his consciousness and his being, and then passed through him and out into the mind and thus the consciousness of humanity both then and for all future generations. The love of the Prophet continues to be a strong, living spiritual emotion among the faithful of Islam, and one of many reasons for this love lies in the fact that through his mind and heart the miracle

13. Mohammed is identified in the Quran as 'the seal of the Prophets,' which effectively closes the book on the descent of knowledge as a revelatory form.

14. A *hadith qudsi*, which is a saying of the Prophet that quotes the direct speech of the Divine Being, was later to relate: 'Someone who reads the Quran is as if he were talking to Me and I were talking to Him.'

of the Quran passed and was made available to the minds and hearts of many generations of faithful Muslims.

(((

THE TRADITIONAL WORLD OF RELIGION, and the genuine expression of a human spirituality always associated with that world, lays a foundation of faith on the principles of knowledge whose origin and source take root in a divine revelation that originates within the all-encompassing knowledge of a Supreme Being Who is the First Cause, the Final End, the Absolute and the One.[15] This knowledge forms the parameters, the substance, and the essence of a knowledge that is identified as the Truth and that represents the true nature of the Reality. It is the vision of the Absolute from the perspective of the Absolute; a Self-Disclosure from the Divine to the human that recalls the primordial revelation[16] and recreates knowledge from the ultimate source. Revelation portrays the physical world as the consequence of actions initiated by the Creator and it offers the study of nature as a virtual science of signs and symbols that reflect the order, design and levels of higher reality that ultimately arrive at the Throne (*al-arsh*) of the Supreme Being. It understands human beings to be thinking beings made in the image of the Divine Being, with a consciousness that both reflects the supreme consciousness and connects with this higher order of Reality. Thus, the Truth has been made manifest to the human mentality in an absolute and unequivocal manner. Because of his free will,

---

15. The Quran officially identifies 99 qualifying Names of God in addition to the reference of other attributes that are implicit in the Quranic text. These 'Names' aid considerably the human mentality in coming to terms with the great unknown and unknowable quality—the factor of mystery—that hovers perennially around the idea of God.

16. The typical point of origin of any well-developed traditional culture was an external revelation, such as Moses for Judaism, Lao-Tzu for Taoism, the Buddha for Buddhism, Jesus for Christianity. Each of these revelations, which contained multiple subtle meanings *ab initio*, both remembered the Primordial Tradition in its essential form and resulted in creating an established 'religion'.

human beings are at liberty to accept, turn to and surrender their minds and hearts to this Supreme Intelligence and this Absolute Being. Human intelligence, supported by both intellect and reason, forms its own conclusion and the expression of a life process becomes sufficient evidence of the validity of a person's choice of purpose and direction.

Today's emphasis on human reason has overshadowed the fact that humanity enjoys another faculty that makes possible the reception of knowledge 'from above', namely the faculty of the intellect, which according to the traditional perspective is the faculty of direct perception and the human repository of the divine knowledge. Needless to say, modern science refuses to recognize the intellect as the receptive faculty of the essential knowledge of God and the filter through which a person can perceive the higher truths, directly as it were, without any intermediary or veil. The human intellect knows in a direct manner, in principle and with an irrefutable certainty, the reality of God and the truths that govern the universe. It is a faculty of perception capable of receiving and reflecting the objective and raw knowledge of the Intellect. The uncreated Quran—the Logos— is the Divine Intellect and this is what the religion means when it refers to the Mind of God being made manifest in the form of revelation, since the Divine Mind or Intellect has become crystallized in the form of an earthly revelation and provides to the subjective, human intellect the objective knowledge it instinctively yearns for.

According to a Holy Tradition,[17] God wrote, with a Mystic Pen that symbolizes the Universal Intellect, the inner reality of all things preserved on the Guarded Tablet before the creation of the world. 'The first of the things Allah created is the Pen (*Qalam*) which He created of Light (*Nur*), and which is made of white pearl; its length is equal to the distance between the sky and the earth. Then He created the Tablet (*al-lawh al-mahfuz*, the guarded tablet), and it is made of white pearl and its surfaces are of red rubies; its length is equal to the distance between the sky and the earth and its width

17. Another tradition, reported by Ibn Abbas, says that 'Allah created the Pen before He created the Creation.' In addition, 'the Pen burst open and the Ink flows from it until the Day of the Resurrection.'

stretches from the East to the West.' The Supreme Pen (*al-qalam al-a'la*) has traditionally been identified with the Universal Intellect, while the ink is the reflection of All-Possibility and results in the possibility of the manifestation of the creation, recalling the Quranic verse: And 'if all the trees on earth were pens and the sea— with seven seas added—[were ink] yet the words of Allah could not be exhausted' (31:27). The Pen also symbolizes the Word, the Logos, in addition to the Universal Intellect, while the Tablet recalls the Universal Substance, so that it can be said that all things are created by the Word. These are the two instruments that bring about and perpetuate the miracle of universal manifestation.

The traditional view in Islam is that there is a celestial Quran (*al-Qur'an al-takwini*) that is uncreated and that there is a written Quran (*al-Qur'an al-tadwini*) whose mode of expression is determined by certain human contingencies so that the Muslims can actually hold the Book in their hands[18] and partake of its knowledge and blessing. The written book that we see within the dimension of this world partakes of a different dimension than any book we have ever known or will know, partly because its substance is not of this world and partly because its inner reality is inimical to this world.

For one thing, the Quran addresses itself directly to the human soul rather than to the human mind, possessing an inner dimension that no literal, philological or literary analysis can reveal. As such, it has powers and properties that do justice to its celestial origin and from there moves into the innermost core of the human entity to give shape and coloration to the fundamental instincts that emanate out of the soul. Through vibration, through sound, through letters, words and phrases that constitute the holy verses of the Book, the divine discourse enters the mind, heart and soul of the believing Muslim as a profound remembrance (*dhikr*) of the Divine Being and the knowledge of the reality that Being represents.

Moreover, it is said that the Book addresses the soul directly because it overwhelms the profane and the earthly with a sense of

18. After the ritual purification, while non-Muslims read translations that have no liturgical value and require no special precaution.

the sacred and the otherworldly, because it casts the absolute and
objective quality of the real upon the relative and subjective aspects
of the world, because it responds to the human yearning for the
Beyond with the plenitude of the Divine Self-disclosure, and
because it brings the presence of the Source and Center into the
world of periphery and contingency that is the human being. This
yearning of the mind and heart for an absolute and definitive
knowledge of God is fundamental to the human soul and lies at the
very heart of all earthly ambition to transcend the broad range of
human limitations through the aid and benevolence of a Supreme
Being as lord and master.

In return for the plenitude of the divine offering, the soul naturally responds to the Object of its ultimate desire. What is it that the
soul desires most and reflects within the mind and heart as the fundamental human aspiration? The great themes of the Quran address
the broad expanse of all human endeavors and enlighten humanity
on all the mysteries of the human condition. The profound doctrinal themes, the great ethical questions, and the sacred sentiments all
reflect the fundamental elements that constitute the human framework of spirituality which must take account of the knowledge
(doctrine), the behavior (ethical morality) and the potential virtue
(ethical action and higher sentiment) of humanity. The trials and
insecurity of life are counterbalanced by the serenity and peace that
is the promise of a person's *islam* (surrender). The uncertainty
reflected in the perennial mystery of life is counterbalanced by the
absolute quality and the certainty that is the lodestone of the word
of God. The imbalance and disequilibrium of the human soul is
counterbalanced by the balance and equilibrium implicit in the
knowledge of the one Reality. The forgetfulness of our self-identity
is counterbalanced by the consciousness of the Greater Self. The
density of the earthly and the mundane is offset by the ethereal
quality of the mystic and the spiritual. The linear quality of the
strictly horizontal perception is animated by the incisive quality of
the vertical disclosure. Finally, the endless diversity and multiplicity
of 'this world' is counterbalanced—indeed resolved—by the unity
and oneness of the Transcendent Center to be encountered in the
'other world'. All these aspects lead toward the development within

the soul of that unity implicit in the human world, the Quranic world and the cosmic world.

Once again, the Holy Quran brings about the existence of another dimension within this world because it is a written as well as a celestial book, capable of being held in the heart as well as the hand of the Muslims. Its exclusive role lies in the manner in which it has become audible and visible, and therefore those who come in contact with it without prejudice, and with a traditional sensibility for the majestic and the sacred, are ready to be the human instrument that is played upon by the divine sound and the visual Arabic letters. The Quran is a sonorous and visual universe that enters the human mentality as forms of audible and visual art that have the power to transform the human form into a living reed, a human calamus and flute, that expresses through man's being and life the very knowledge of God. Psalmody is the first art of Islam, while the second major art is calligraphy,[19] constituting the letters and words of the Book and reflecting on the earthly plane the writing on the Guarded Tablet. Psalmody manifests the sound and modulation of the verses while calligraphy is a sacred art that humans carry within themselves from the inception of the revelation since 'He taught man with the Pen, taught man what he knew not' (96:4–5).

The physical presence of the Quran is not in the pages and binding as with other books, but rather in its resonant splendor and its calligraphic majesty. Muslims read the Quran for the knowledge, guidance and truth implicit in the words and verses; but they also read the verses because they contain a 'spiritual presence' through the recitation and intonation of the divine speech that literally brings them into the Presence of God. When a Muslim recites the verses orally, he hears firstly himself reciting the words, then by way of extension he hears the voice of the Prophet through whom the Quran passed into the world of people, and finally he hears the

19. 'Calligraphy is the basic art of creation of points and lines in an endless variety of forms and rhythms which never cease to bring about recollection (*tidhkar* or *dhikr*) of the Primordial Act of the Divine Pen for those who are capable of contemplating in forms the trace of the Formless.' S.H. Nasr, *Islamic Art and Spirituality* (Albany, NY: SUNY Press, 1987), p19

voice of God through the very words of God, and these sounds create a feeling of proximity of the Divine Presence that emanate from within the text. The Muslim who reads the sacred verses over and over on a daily basis can create within his mind and heart a measured, auditory rhythm that is based on sacred rhythms embedded within the letters and words of the text itself. In turn, these rhythms create an inner harmony that amounts to 'an echo in the minds and world of the men who read it, and returns them to a state in which they participate in its paradisal joy and beauty. Herein lies its alchemical effect.'[20]

For the purposes of worship, the chanted Quran is the prototype of all worship through sacred sound. It is a kind of divine music that overlays the human soul with knowledge of origins, purpose and ultimate end and provides the guidance that will lead people in the right direction on the way of return to God. The sonorous character of the Quranic revelation remains central to the spiritual life of Islam. Through recitation and as a means of worshipping Allah, the sacred, rhythmic presence is felt by Arab and non-Arab Muslims alike, including Persian, Turkish, African, Indian and the Malays of Malaysia and Indonesia, all of whom do not use Arabic as a mother tongue. In fact, the majority of Muslims are non-Arabic, even though Islam is assumed to be a thoroughly Arabic or Arabized religion.

The Quran contains a certain majesty, harmony, rhythm and flow that pours out from the sacred text and cannot be translated without seriously altering the nature of the profound sacredness that emanates from the spiritual presence contained within the letters and sounds. There is a majestic projection of sound that is primordial, central and eternal; primordial in that the sound and meaning resort back to the source and remembers origins; central because it brings humanity immediately back from the periphery of their earthly existence to the very center of their being; eternal because it lifts the reciter out of the march of a lateral, advancing time to the eternal now, the sacred present, that transcends and extinguishes the temporal march of time with its window into eternity.

20. Ibid., p77.

Quranic recitation determines the framework and progress of the spiritual life for all Muslims. They draw upon the language of the Quran to give a spiritual frame to their hopes, fears, sorrows, regrets, and aspirations. They use the Quran as a means of withdrawing for a few moments during the course of the day, whether it is in the early morning when the birds sing their own sacred verses, or after the sunset prayer when the calm of dusk merges into the stillness of night. The holy recitation relieves the mind, the psyche, and the soul of those who intone the verses from the gravitational pull of this world with its implicit imbalance, disharmony and lack of peace. When the Muslims arise in the morning at the call to prayer, they have available the sacred book that contains all they need to know and therefore they possess the means to realize that knowledge in their daily lives. Small wonder then that devout Muslims turn to the Holy Quran for sustenance and strength on a daily basis throughout the course of their lives, a turning that precludes all doubt and despair and leads their inner being back to the center and source of their existence within the Divine Being.

(((

REVELATION BRINGS A DOCTRINE that conveys a meaning, a morality that establishes a purpose and spiritual sensibilities that lead to a virtuous life culminating in the perfection of the soul and a consciousness fully united with the knowledge of God. The depth and profundity of the knowledge of the Origin, the Real, the Truth, the Supreme Intelligence, and the One Reality, given its abundant luminescence and spiritual consequences for humanity, cannot be known and realized without the descent of a supernatural communication whose divinely inspired text neutralizes all mystery and whose theurgic radiation suffuses the mind, heart and soul with its radiance (*al-nur*) and blessing (*al-baraka*).

The Quran has alternatively been described as a Recitation (*al-qur'an*), a Discernment (*al-furqan*), the mother of all books (*umm al-kitab*), the essential Guidance (*al-huda*), the perennial wisdom (*hikmah*), and the ultimate remembrance (*dhikr*). Its very name

Recitation (*qur'an*) recalls the manner in which it was delivered, the way it was received and remembered, and the means with which it is treasured and preserved, for the Qur'an is a reading and a recitation first and foremost, a book of verses and the word of God on the tongues of the faithful. As a criterion and discernment, it establishes once and for all time the true nature of the Real as opposed to the unreal, the light of truth overshadowing the darkness of falsehood and ignorance. The Quranic guidance shapes all personal and ethical conduct and gives definition to the actions of the believers who would not always know otherwise how to behave in the light of their true desires; while its wisdom becomes an internalized knowledge within the heart and ultimately manifests itself back out into the world as virtue.

As Divine Remembrance, however, the Quran is the ultimate sacred psychology, leading the human soul[21] back from the periphery to the Center and establishing the doctrinal knowledge and the sacred sentiments necessary for the soul's journey of return to the Divine Fold. The Quran is identified as the *dhikr Allah* that is also one of the names of the Prophet and remembers the Quranic verse: 'Nothing is greater than the remembrance of God' (29:45). Its living presence, that manifests as a kind of spiritual perfume within the mind, focuses the human consciousness on 'the one thing needful' and recreates the ambiance of primordial beatitude that constituted the primordial consciousness of Adam before the fall from the Paradise.

The interaction of human consciousness and Divine Remembrance is subtle and intricate. The very *raison d'etre* of the human consciousness is to realize within the individual self the knowledge of the Universal Self. Remembrance, then, whether it is through the Profession of Faith in the Islamic *Shahadah*, in the repetition of the Name of God through the ceremony of prayer, or the experience of the Quran through its recitation, activates the human consciousness with the living presence of the Divinity. To enjoy a conscious-

---

21. The soul can be considered the summary of all of man's faculties, the ground of his being and the theater in which his essence is expressed and made manifest.

ness of the individual self without the possibility of connecting to the Supreme Self is: To roam on the periphery rather than be at the center, to live in an evanescent rather than a transcending world, and to recognize a fundamental mystery at the heart of existence, while denying its true origin and source.

The Quran, as Divine Discourse and Revelatory Word, remains the ultimate source of knowledge, the wellspring of all morality and ethics, and the means of spiritual worship that permits people to transcend their limitations and approach the true knowledge of the Reality as a Truth and as a Presence. It can be summarized in three distinct ways. Firstly, it represents a doctrine containing the metaphysical knowledge of God and the science of reality concerning the ultimate nature of things and of the true reality. Secondly, it presents an ethical code of conduct as the basis of an Islamic law. One of the purposes of revelation is to ground the morality of humanity within the precinct of a sacred knowledge that has the power to deliver a truth that is absolute as well as real and that finds its source and efficacy beyond the whims of human society. The revelation provides a moral foundation that transcends the subjectivity of humanity with an objectivity that finds its root into the authority and command of a Supreme Being. Thirdly, the Word of God offers the narrative content of a sacred and perennial history that transcends linear time by appealing to the very sensitivities of the human soul, a sacred history of the soul that casts in cameo the great personages of Biblical and Quranic history, from messengers and prophets to pharaohs, conquerors and kings. In recounting the strengths and limitations of the great figures of sacred history, the Quran teaches humanity a wide range of moral and spiritual principles. These sacred narratives appeal directly to the human soul because it is ultimately within the ground of the soul that the battle is fought between the forces of good and evil and between the virtuous and the profane life, forces that highlight the tendencies of the soul in its struggle to overcome the contingencies of existence. To become aware of the currents of a sacred history is to become aware of the history of one's own soul, for humankind was made from *one soul* and enjoys a unique human nature that is as changeless as it is enduring.

The descent of the knowledge of God in the form of a metaphysical doctrine, a moral law and a sacred chronicle of the soul remains the one true source we have available for an absolute expression of an Absolute Truth. The ascent of the spiritual aspiration and experience of humanity based on the knowledge of God remains the one true means we still have available to transcend our limitations and perfect ourselves. Knowledge descends as sacred speech because Allah is the Living, the Knowing, the Willing, and the All-powerful. Consequently, humans can make their journey of ascent and return to God because these divine attributes are reflected within their theomorphic nature as Life, Knowledge, Free Will, and Power that find their expression ultimately through speech. Because of the revelation, we live as being who have access to the essential knowledge, who choose what we wish to believe, who put our beliefs into practice through the force of an inner power in order to actualize and ultimately realize this knowledge resulting from our initial choice. Finally, through the speech of worship, we can actualize the encounter of the human with the Divine to counterbalance the sacred encounter of the Divine with the human made possible through the descent of revelation.

PART B

THE UNIVERSAL BODY OF GOD

To read the book of Nature is to read the message of the traditional symbols that constitute the forms and elements of that nature. Through a willingness to partake of the symbolist spirit and through an appreciation of the value and significance of the traditional symbols in revelation and within nature, we can still have access to the original sources of knowledge that reflect higher states of being and of reality, and thus we can still hope to know, however indirectly, 'the one thing needful'.

IV

MAN AGAINST
THE LAST HORIZON

Pass world! I am the dreamer that remains;
the man clear cut against the last horizon.
(*The Lost World of the Kalahari*, Laurens van der Post)

THE ISLAMIC TRADITIONS insist that the resolution to life's perennial mystery lies just beyond the border of two horizons, the near
horizon existing within the human being and the distant horizon
encircling the known world. As such, true believers need only open
their minds and hearts to these outer and inner messages in order to
develop a profound affinity for the knowledge implicit in the symbols within nature and the wisdom that is internalized within the
ground experience of the human soul. The Quran is very specific
and clear on this point. 'Soon We shall show them Our signs on the
horizon and within their own souls until it becomes clear to them
that this is the Truth' (41:53). The answer to the cosmic question lies
at the center and on the edge, at the center of the human being and
on the edge of the known world. The certainty that we desperately
desires is never fully at hand, and neither is the happiness and peace
that is a latent promise of the human condition symbolized in the
perennial image of the Paradise; but the knowledge that we need to
realize in order to perfect our entity and fulfil our vocation lies
within the inmost depths of our being and on the horizon of the
known world.

Whether near or distant, the image of the horizon always leads humanity into the mythical region of 'beyond'. It lies out of reach of the human body, but always within sight of the human mind with its eternal message of aspiration and hope. Wherever we turn, we come face to face with the horizon. The separation of heaven and earth highlighted by the image of the horizon confronts us daily with its compelling and inscrutable mystery. The horizon marks the defining edge of the visible world; in this realm of beyond resides the mystique of a deep, dark secret. The horizon invites, challenges, and ultimately excludes us with the questions it raises and the answers it withholds, a cosmic divide between terrestrial and celestial worlds. As such, it remains the perennial and permanent image of the fundamental duality that defines this world.

Whether we behold the vast dome of the heavens with its array of color, clouds and celestial objects, or regard the great expanse of an earth, 'how it is spread out' (88:20) like a carpet, the magnificent picture of Heaven and earth remains split into two unequal halves that nothing can reconcile save the unifying principle of the Divinity who has created and sustains the totality of the metacosmic universe. The horizon beckons humankind as the first tier of the unseen reality. It cuts across the divided self of our consciousness just as it tears through the reality of this world with its promise of unknown worlds and alternative realities. The horizon forms the circumference of the known world and marks the great Celestial Divide that exists between Heaven and Earth.[1] These two domains belong solely to God, a truth that is sorely forgotten during these times. They are, according to the Quranic revelation, 'My Heaven' and 'My Earth'.[2]

On the one hand, the sacred speech of the Quran declares that 'truly, My Earth is spacious' (29:56). It is spread out in every direction unto the earthly horizon and provides ample space for the believers to worship and serve the Divinity. The empyreal sky

---

1. One relies on capital letters in certain instances to emphasize the universal and symbolic nature of the terminology whose profound impact transcends the limited perspective of the everyday world.

2. 'It is He Who is God in heaven and God on earth, and He is full of Wisdom, the All-Knowing' (43:84).

above, on the other hand, in its simple grandeur and awesome magnitude, gives every indication of the multi-layered heavens portrayed in scripture as the primordial and post mortal paradise, the final abode of the faithful, 'Enter thou, then, among my devotees! Yea, enter thou My Heaven!' (89:30) God's personal domain spreads as a celestial dome over the earth and reaches down in a gesture of touching simplicity as it meets the earth at every point along the horizon. 'He created the heavens without any pillars that you can see; He set on the earth mountains standing firm, lest it should shake with you' (31:10).

The earth remains forever as the land of spaciousness and firm stability; the heavens remain forever the empyrean of great magnitude and infinitude. The sky, as the gateway to the universe and 'the canopy raised high' (52:5), confronts the human eye as the vault of heaven and the firmament of the Divinity in all of its majesty and mystery. 'Such is the creation of Allah' and, inquiringly, the Divine I asks about the supra-personal Him: Now 'show Me what is there that others besides Him have created?' (31:11) Such is the creation of God that the horizon separates these two worlds into two unequal halves of the cosmic unity: the one earthly, natural, and finite; the other celestial, supra-natural, and infinite. The prosaic narrative of a primordial Adam is portrayed against the backdrop of infinite space and the cosmic drama of the heavenly spheres. 'It is Allah Who has created the heavens and the earth and all that is between them in six days. Then He established Himself on the Throne' (32:4).

We commenced this Part with reflections on the image of the horizon because it is a sacred and traditional symbol whose ultimate message highlights and transcends the limitations of the horizons found within both humanity and the world. Deep beyond the thin veneer of this world lies a fundamental interrogative that sets the foundation to the human inquiry into the meaning of the human identity and its place in the world, and this question is no better summarized than in the image of the distant horizon. Similarly, at the heart of the spirit of humanity exists a fundamental mystery whose explanation lies forever beyond the near horizon of the human soul, unattainable yet assessable, unfathomable yet intelligible to the human mind, ready to be known and realized through the intelligence[3] and spiritual sentiments of the human heart. This mystery exists as the prime motivating force of the spirit to transcend the limitations of the purely human condition and the earthly sphere through the inner spirit that lies at the heart of all form.

We find ourselves in time and space, living in the existential condition of a particular world, and this condition implies a dual axis, the one existential and horizontal and the other spiritual and vertical. The image of the horizon is an image of place and time, both finite and temporal. It is there wherever we turn as the encompassing and horizontal remembrance of earthly finitude. The horizon contains a vertical implication by virtue of what lies ultimately beyond it. As a primordial image of majesty and mystery, the horizon confronts us with its metacosmic projection of the Divine Being as both the Truth and the Reality (*al-Haqq*). The Quran confirms this in multiple verses: 'To God belongs the East and the West. Everywhere you turn, there is the Face of God' (2:115) and 'He is Lord of the East and the West; there is no God but He' (73:9). The horizon challenges us to expand our limited and narrow vision, to reach beyond our microcosmic selves and to rise like the sun, moon and stars over the horizon of our inner beings through the consciousness and remembrance of God that activates both the human spirit and the spirit of the world. The presence of the horizon marks the separation of seen and unseen worlds and serves as a remembrance and a hope to transcend the boundaries of these external and inner worlds.

The meaning implicit in the horizon challenges the modern mentality of people today with its clear message of mystery beyond the rim of the known world, 'He alone knows the Unseen, nor does He make anyone acquainted with His mysteries' (72:26), and the secret just beyond the horizon of the inner self, 'Say: 'The (Quran) was sent down by Him Who knows the Mystery in the heavens and the earth: verily He is Oft-Forgiving, Most Merciful' (25:6). The traditional peoples of earlier ages responded to the mystery within

---

3. In the Islamic perspective, the seat of the intelligence lies in the heart as a faculty of discernment for all that is real and true. The Prophet of Islam is recorded in the Holy Traditions as having said: 'God has created nothing more noble than intelligence, and His wrath is on him who despises it.'

the universe and the secret within themselves with humility and interest because they knew and were prepared to believe in what the scriptures asserted, namely that the mystery implicit in the outer and inner horizon has always inspired the human mind to reach beyond the visible world and the inner self through aspiration and yearning. People down through the ages have always wondered what lay beyond the thin thread that marks the end of the known world. The aura of mystery that emanates from the other side of the horizon reaches in and virtually seizes all aspects of the human entity, including the physical, the emotional, the psychic and ultimately the higher spiritual levels of human manifestation with its hidden attraction and subtle lure.

History has already recorded the exploits of those adventurers who crossed seas, traversed deserts, and climbed mountains in order to expand the horizons of the known world and to broaden the physical knowledge of the unknown world beyond the horizon. For humanity throughout history, the mystery of the unknown always lay in wait beyond the physical, the literal horizon, an area held in great awe by most primitive peoples who had no idea what lay beyond the visual perspective of their horizon. As far as they were concerned, the horizon marked the terminus of the earth. Beyond their horizon lay demons and dragons that populated the netherworld of the earth. For more imaginative adventurers such as Columbus and Vasco de Gama, it held the possibility and lure of discovering new routes, new worlds and/or lost continents. For the majority of peoples of earlier times, the horizon ultimately represented the end of the earth beyond which a person would simply fall off the world. It is not surprising then that the symbolic image of the horizon has always fascinated humankind down through the ages.

The horizon has traditionally appealed to virtually every aspect of our inner make up, including the mind, psyche, emotions and sacred instincts. From the point of view of the human mind, the horizon has always held an appeal as a source of inspiration for intellectual curiosity. The mystery beyond the horizon was unknown and possibly unreachable, yet curiously accessible in principle by becoming a symbol of hope and aspiration. It stirred the imagination of the traditional active mind in search of the new, the enigmatic and the mysterious. From the point of view of the psyche, the mystery implicit in the horizon drew upon secret messages from the realms of the unconscious. Within the psychic plane, the mystery is all that is abstract and all that is unseen; it lay beyond the image of the horizon as a latent and enduring possibility. The mystery permeates the realm of the subconscious and the subterranean caverns of the human ego, resurrecting primal desires and formulating central questions in search of answers.

From the viewpoint of the human emotions, the mystery implicit in the horizon manifests itself within humankind as the 'secret' (*assirr*), and this secret is none other than a niche, a grotto, or a holy cave of sacred feeling that is intuitive and untaught. This secret manifests itself as a sacred feeling that reaches out and makes itself known to the mind and psyche in order to communicate beyond its own limited confines and ultimately to worship that which is greater than itself. Finally, the horizon appeals directly to the instinctive spiritual ambiance that is centered within the human being and that resides within the soul as the vertical axis representing all that is eternal, infinite and sublime. The human soul recognizes and responds instinctively to the implicit meaning behind this metacosmic symbol. The image of the near horizon within us is the touchstone through which we define the world, and the symbol of the celestial divide through which we seek the essential knowledge of God.

(((

THE SYMBOLIC IMAGE of the horizon is a permanent reminder to humanity of the absolute chasm that exists between the terrestrial world we inhabit and the celestial realm of the universe that provides the permanent backdrop to our temporary, makeshift reality. It marks the profound and absolute separation of the earth and the heavens, of time and the timeless, of the finite and the infinite. The horizon clearly defines the distinction between the earthly environment spread out before us, the blue dome of the day-time sky and the nocturnal 'city of God' illuminating the night sky. As such, the horizon is a profoundly graphic image that bears no misunderstanding in its meaning or its message. We live within the confines of the earth, within time, within the finitude of our existence. As the hem of the earth's garment and borderland of the known world, the horizon is the perennial symbol of the separation that exists between the relative world of humanity and the absolute world of God, between the world of matter on this side of the horizon and the world of the spirit beyond the horizon.

Its pervasive presence cuts across the known universe with a line that encircles the entire visual world. We see its definitive image. We feel its comprehensive presence. We live within its borders, for the horizon represents a threshold beyond which we do not step without entering realms of mystery and imagination. We live in a world of horizons, both inner as well as external that shape and color our understanding of self and our vision of the world. The horizon is within us; just as we are reflected in profile against the last known horizon. It encourages us to leave behind our narrow and limited perspective of self. It challenges us to raise our expectations for what we hope to achieve: to lift the veils that keep us guessing about the true nature of reality and to expand the horizons of our mind and heart in search of the unseen mystery that always characterizes the 'beyond-ness' on the other side of the horizon.

The promise of the horizon lies behind its visible face. The proverbial pot of gold may lie at the end of the rainbow[4] as a subjective desire, but the rainbow itself, which spans the length of the horizon and disappears into its mysterious depths, is an objective fact, even though it is clearly not a material phenomenon. The sun rises over the horizon of our world as a sustenance and a light, and sets below the rim of the horizon in its perennial cycle of departure and return.

4. 'The rainbow is a symbol of the fleeting beauty of the human world, in whose transience is manifested eternal laws that ever afresh create the wonder of existence. In other words, the rainbow becomes the symbol of the ungraspable essence of reality, which eludes us in our world of seemingly firm objects and hard facts. It is a phenomenon that always arouses deep feelings in us, even if we have seen it a thousand times before. It astonishes us and fills us with joy and admiration, if not with religious awe, or else it becomes for us an omen of profound importance.' Lama Anagarika Govinda, *Buddhist Reflections* (York Beach, ME: Samuel Weiser, 1991), p190.

Yet, the sacred image of the sun hovering over the horizon at dawn means more than its literal truth, since it arrives at each moment in time as a holy assurance that the eternal beginning of hope, of possibility and of promise awaits the coming of every dawn.

In fact, the message of transcendence is traced along the line of the horizon. Ultimately, the logical consequence of the separation, hope and promise implicit in the symbol of the horizon must be the union of the human being with the Divinity, a Divine Being who has created humanity as His 'thinking creation'. The fundamental aspiration of the human entity is to return to the paradise lost, to reunite the loved one with the Beloved, to transcend the limitations of the human entity and to fulfill and perfect the human soul in its evolution and journey of return to the Divinity. Transcendence is engraved on the human soul as a sacred yearning of the creature for the Creator, and it is written throughout the natural and visible world as a fundamental mystery whose meaning and magic lie in its power to draw the human being out of the strictly human condition and beyond the known universe through forms of communication such as revelation and symbolic imagery that permit intimacy and sacred sentiment with the Supreme Being, who is identified in the revelation as the Holy One (*Al-Qudus*) and the Only One (*Al-Ahad*).

In addition to the promise of transcendence and union, the symbolic image of the horizon also inspires the vision of two journeys, the one within the external world and the other within the inner world, both amounting to journeys that lead into the dark interior beyond the horizon. The first journey is the external one that seeks out natural wilderness and unexplored frontiers anywhere in order to map the limits of the earth, the other an inward journey toward an inner horizon that becomes the model for the spiritual journey of the soul in its quest of return to the Divinity.[5] In order to enter

---

5. The prototype of the outer and inner journey is exemplified in the life of the Prophet Mohammed. The *hegira* of the Prophet from Makkah to Medinah represents the way of exile and return that every soul must pass through in this life and that the Prophet actually performed in real life as model and example to future generations. The inner journey is exemplified in the *mi'raj*, or night journey that took the Prophet through the seven heavens unto the very Throne of God and thus provides all Muslims with the supreme prototype of the soul's spiritual journey to God.

the spiritual realms that are promised beyond the horizon, we must make a journey into the interior of the self in search of knowledge and experience that can help us in this journey of return toward unity. The traditional imagery of the journey and the way has been highlighted down through the ages in the major world religions, such as Taoism, in which the Tao is none other than a Way of Life, and reminiscent of Christ's well-known observation in which he proclaimed 'I am the Way, the Truth, and the Light,' and ever mindful of the emphasis on the 'straight path' within Islam and of the *tariqa* or 'way of return' of the Sufis.

The journey into the interior initially calls to mind the earthly journeys that culminated in the 19th century, when the great European adventurers ventured into the unexplored regions of central Africa in search of what at that time was the mythological source of the Nile, the nearly mythical journeys of Stanley, Burton and Livingston. Those expeditions were real, overland journeys conducted in an age and place in which virgin territory still needed to be discovered, explored, and opened up for growth and development. Epic journeys have been made down through history and within literature, such as the legendary wanderings of Odysseus and the search for the Holy Grail, the journeys of Columbus in search of an alternative route to China, or Marco Polo and Ibn Batutta in search of the silk and spice routes into the East. Journeys have been made to scale the heights of the Himalayas and to explore the vast and barren wastes of Antarctica. More recently, we have ventured into space, set foot upon the moon and sent out space probes to explore the nearby planets of our immediate solar system.

Yet none of these journeys will ever compare to the challenges that are implicit in the journey into the dark and mysterious interior of the human being, a journey that will lead into the only genuine and truly final frontier left to explore, a frontier that still contains all the secrets and mystery of human origins and the ultimate source of knowledge, making the wonder and fascination that gripped humanity for 2,000 years concerning the source of the Nile pale by comparison. Nothing will be able to compare with the inward journey toward the near horizon, beyond which lies the knowledge of perfection and the secret of human transcendence.

Once again, the Quranic verse that refers to God's 'signs' within the self and on the horizon echoes here, since knowledge of the self represents the last frontier for humans to conquer, reflecting the words of the Prophet: 'He who known himself knows His Lord.'

More than ever before, we need to turn within and examine the frontiers of the spirit that lie embedded within our minds, our psyche, our intuition, and our souls. We have drifted far away from our source in the Divine Proximity and from our center in the Divine Oneness and Unity. From the spiritual point of view, we are no longer child prodigies in the infancy of time. We are no longer direct, spontaneous or innerly free, and we no longer express the naturalness and intuitive spontaneity that comes from instinctive and spiritual living. We no longer have the face of the child who shows the world with delightful and disarming candor the pure impulses of the human soul. In many ways, the child exists as the prototype of a truly spiritual human being. In the child's curiosity, instincts and natural expression of living lies the secret of all metaphysics.

As we become older, we lose this natural sheen of childhood's simplicity, while the open face of infancy disappears from view behind a mask of contemporary thinking and a veil of sophisticated living. We develop earthly knowledge and lose the natural instincts of an essential and spiritual knowledge. Out of the poetry of our infancy emerges the prosaic narrative of adulthood which amounts to a fiction in which the main characters play out their roles using a false mask, out of touch with all true instincts and unwilling to expose the true self that still lies embedded within the shell of people living in today's modern world. The final stage of life inevitably turns into a prosaic elegy of disappointment and regret, out of touch with the true person within—the archetype True Man according to the Taoists—and out of contact with the one reality that can give life meaning, whether it be infancy, childhood, adulthood, or declining old age.

From the spiritual point of view, we are presently living in the old age of our time, on a horizon that is virtually at the edge of a known world, beyond which lies nothing but an abyss of oblivion. We are fragmented and on the periphery of ourselves, living on the surface of the world and content with surface images. We have no center

because we are no longer in contact with the center within ourselves, which coincides with the Center of the cosmic universe at
whose core is the Lord of all the worlds (*rabb il-a'lamin*). As a civilization,[6] we have created a deep chasm between the duality of our
two existing worlds, the manifested and sentient world that humans
experience and the intuitive and transcendental world of the spirit.
We live in a purely secular and solitary world rather than the comprehensive universe that was envisioned within the traditional perspective,[7] a world whose members actively deny all possibility of the
supernatural and neutralize the infinite subtlety of the world of the
spirit through its mundane understanding of the spirit of the world.
The sacred formula in Islam and the testament of faith, namely the
revered *shahadah* of the Muslims, remains a fundamental denial of
the lasting value of this world for the sake of an ultimate affirmation
of the one Reality.

The *shahadah* is a sacred formula of Islam that denies the world in
order to affirm the one God. The contemporary mantra espousing
the death of God has become an overwhelming negation that verifies
the world at the expense of the Divinity. In fully accepting the
secularist perspective and actively disbelieving the knowledge of God
and the kind of reality implicit in this knowledge, we have reduced
the mystery that surrounds both *Homo sapiens* and the human
understanding of the world to a potentially solvable enigma. Within
the modern perspective, in its encasement of a purely material and
sense-oriented science, the search for knowledge has become the
search for ever more specialized accumulations of information in

6. 'Our culture is superficial today, and our knowledge dangerous, because we
are rich in mechanisms and poor in purposes. The balance of mind which once
came of a warm religious faith is gone; science has taken from us the supernatural
bases of our morality, and all the world seems consumed in a disorderly individual-
ism that reflects the chaotic fragmentation of our character.' Will Durant, *The Pleasures of Philosophy* (New York: Simon Schuster, 1981), p xii.

7. It is noteworthy that the English word 'universe' derives from the Latin word
niversus (meaning whole) which further breaks down into *nus* (one) + *versus*, this
being the past participle of the verb *vetere*, which curiously and perhaps fittingly
means 'to turn', thus the word universe itself, derives from an earlier context that
found its root in the centrifugal turning (*versus*) of the whole (*niversus*) as a unity
(*nus*).

the form of facts that can be identified as real and therefore true, although what the meaning of real and true is within this context is anyone's guess. In the traditional perspective, knowledge pursued as a science was a means to an end, in which individuals and their society could come closer in understanding and experience to the Lord of all the worlds. The knowledge pursued by modern science has become a limited knowledge of observable facts, a knowledge that has turned into an end in itself, without the ability to sub-stantiate any meaning beyond the surface data it uncovers.

We need to re-examine the contents of our fundamental intui-tions. There are a number of truths that we need to re-establish and re-affirm if we are going to successfully come to terms with the human condition in the new age of the millennium. As the 'human' race, we cannot forever remain as adolescents, pretending that we know or worse believing that there are things that we need not know. In truth, everything we need to know is accessible to us, through revelation, common sense, conscience, and what the body tells us through the physical senses. While it is true that the range of knowledge is infinite, the essential knowledge we need in order to function as human beings within the earthly environment is imme-diate and accessible to one and all and is not the purview of the sci-entific elite. The human heart can contain the truth, and in our heart of hearts, we are capable of knowing truth's truth. In other words, in our essence, we can know the Essence.[8] That is the prom-ise implicit in the image of the horizon and the meaning that lies beyond its symbolic presence.

(((

8. A Holy Tradition (*hadith qudsi*) of the Prophet phrases this thought in another way: 'Neither in the earth nor in the heavens is there space for Me, but in the heart of my believing servant there is space for Me.' Within the Christian tradi-tion, Meister Eckhart has written: 'God might make numberless heavens and earths, yet these...would be of less extent than a middle point compared with the standpoint of a soul attuned to God.'

THE SYMBOL OF THE DISTANT HORIZON is both an illusion and a paradox, an illusion because it is a phantom mirage that presents itself as a distinct reality and a paradox because its message combines contradictory aspects of both separation and unity. Let us consider this more closely because it is important to understand that implicit in the horizontal plane is the vertical axis that leads to the gateway to the inspiration of faith and the consequences of spiritual experience.

At first glance, as in a one-dimensional drawing, if we gaze out at the graphic image of the place where earth and sky meet, the horizontal line issuing forth through this picture of heaven and earth disappears into a seamless totality and does not appear as the hem of the world that we know it to be. The separation of heaven and earth, in the form of a great horizontal fissure dividing the expansive spread of the earth and the monumental canopy of the heavens, becomes a seam in the fabric of the visible world only when the sun, moon and stars rise and set behind the all-defining horizon. 'It is He who made the sun to be a shining glory and the moon to be a light (of beauty), and measured out stages for it: that ye might know the number of years and the count (of time)' (10:5). Then, this seamless whole is cracked into two parts and we are welcomed into the definition of the earthly sphere surrounded by the magnitude of the heavens. Then, we behold a finite world below in an infinite universe that extends above and beyond.

For all of its multiple messages, the horizon ultimately makes the world finite and reminds us of our finitude. We feel this finitude within the horizon of our own being as a permanent mark of the human condition. The Quran affirms that the signs of the absolute truth lie 'on the horizon' and 'within their own souls' (41:53), but as part of the human condition, there exists an unreality that lies along the great fissure of the horizon and within the deep chasm that exists within ourselves. This seeming unreality commences as an incomplete awareness of ourselves and our true nature, and thrives on the myths and illusions that we propagate about ourselves at the expense of the whole. Out of this chasm of unreality emerge the two halves of ourselves, just as over the horizon emerges the duality of the world.

Nevertheless, the message of the horizon remains forever two-fold. While the horizon sets limits and exists as the hem of the world, at the same time this graphic image of the earth within the universe appears as a seamless whole whose symbolic imagery remembers and invokes the wholeness and the unity that exists as the central and unifying reality of the Divinity. Transcendence awaits us on the other side of the horizon. It is always there, alluring the human mind with its message of promise and hope. Similarly, the possibility of transcendence lies within our beings and expresses itself as a fundamental human impulse to yearn for the greater whole that overlays the divided self. This promise desires to climb out of and reach beyond the limiting confines of the individual ego, enclosed as it is in its own centralizing egocentricity, in order to arrive at the center of the self, the center of the world, indeed the Center of the Universe.

In order to approach the challenge implicit in transcendence, the human entity is well equipped with a number of attributes and faculties that not only make us unique individuals within creation but also provides us with the means to fulfill the human vocation. Through the higher faculty of the intellect, people can know of God directly. Through mind, they can conceive of the Divinity as a living Reality. Through intelligence, they can contemplate the thought and propel it to action. Through consciousness, they can bring this Presence down into their conscious reckoning whenever they choose. Through free will, they can act upon the wishes of the Divinity and surrender their will to the supreme Will of God, this being the essence and goal of the religion of Islam. This knowledge and this desire, in the form of surrender, hovers over the near horizon of the inner self, and thus humanity is encompassed within the circle of our inner horizon.

Human beings represent perfection, at least in principle if not in actuality. They are called true man according to the Taoists, Adam Kadmon or primordial man in the Kabbalah, the completed man according to the Muslims, as a complement to the perfected man of the primordial tradition. As God's thinking creation, humans have a mind that can conceive of God as knowledge and therefore they can share in the Divine wisdom that is the result of that knowledge.

They have a will that can desire the Divinity and that therefore can unite the human will with the Divine Will through perfect surrender. They have a heart that can contain the Divinity and therefore can establish a holy intimacy with the Divinity through a variety of sacred sentiments. Finally, they have a soul/spirit that reflects the Divine Spirit and that therefore can enter the Sacred Presence as a single soul within the unifying Spirit of God. Every thought, every desire, every sacred emotion and every emanation of soul serves as a remembrance of God and therefore permits an awareness of the totality that comes with a conscious attachment with the Divine Being. The two halves of the self and the duality implicit in the horizon find their unity in the Divine Being. Otherwise, there is no alternative other than to run the risk of being a divided self living in a superficial and surface world whose horizon represents, not the edge of the known world but its virtual end point, beyond which a person would simply fall off into the abyss.

Humans live in a borderland between heaven and earth and therefore their human condition creates its own horizon. Nothing could be nearer to them than this inner divide, except of course the Divinity itself who is 'nearer to you than your jugular vein' (50:16). Two distinct selves emerge within the near horizon, the one concerned with living in this world and coping with the reality of daily existence, the other concerned with confronting the reality of the world of the spirit and interested in having a genuine experience of spirituality that is the human manifestation of that reality. We live and experience the world both horizontally and vertically, horizontally concerning all that pertains to the senses, the lower emotions and the cognitive mind; vertically concerning all that pertains to the higher emotions, to intuitive mind, to a synthesizing consciousness and to the uplifting perfume of the virtues.

Exploration of the inner frontier of the human spirit is the final frontier of humanity. We draw upon the image of the frontier in making reference to the inner person in order to emphasize the importance of our inner world for us as modern and contemporary individuals, particularly during this time period when we are on the threshold of a new century and millennium. It is necessary more than ever to turn within and examine precisely where we stand within our beings as regards the Truth, the Knowledge, and the Wisdom that demands to be acknowledged during these times, if for no other reason than because we desperately need the knowledge of the truth and its accompanying wisdom to guide us through the new stages of life that we will soon be confronted with. Every frontier, and especially the inner human frontier with its landscape of mind, psyche, consciousness and spiritual intuition, can be characterized as a hinterland and wilderness that modern people still need to explore and more fully experience. Every frontier contains the mystique of an all-pervading mystery and this reflects the fundamental mystery that all humans are faced with, a mystery that we must recognize for what it is if we are to preserve any kind of humility in light of the Divine Magnitude and Unity.

The human frontier as final frontier is still an unknown and unmapped region open for exploration and discovery. We need to recognize the fact that it exists within us as a source of knowledge, a well of potential experience, and a means of verification until, as the Quran asserts, 'it becomes manifest to them that this is the truth' (41:53). We need to explore the many possibilities of this inner landscape through an active exploration of our inner beings. In the face of this unknown inner frontier, all modern-day explanations break down and all theoretical speculations that serve as the philosophical commentary of the scientific perspective fail to deliver the one thing essential, namely clarity of mind, intuition of heart and certitude of soul. At the threshold of the inner frontier, we are suspended between two worlds, the one being the physical world of experience and the other the cerebral world of knowing combined with the psychic world of reflective consciousness. To look within in search of a better understanding of self and in response to the traditional wisdom 'know thyself' represents a moment of pure awakening. Such a moment has always been recognized by the traditions as a condition that is more spiritual than psychological and the *conditio sine qua non* of the true spiritual experience.

To meet the challenge of this unknown frontier is primarily intuitive rather than cognitive and as such it opens the individual onto the plane of spiritual instincts and the sacred emotions that are embedded within the landscape of this uncharted territory. It is not the response to a new scientific explanation, a new paradigm of knowledge, a new age spirituality or even a new religion that could melt the heart, expand the horizon of our mentalities, or fuse the soul with certitude and certainty, in order to arrive at tranquility and serenity of the spirit. The journey into the interior of the human frontier can in fact create a new range of human experience for the unknown mystery that lies at the heart of all knowledge, an experience that will expose all fantasies about ourselves and the myths of our existing world for what they really are, namely peripheral encounters and surface phenomena that in no way penetrate the depths of the mind, heart and soul—a mind that knows, a heart that desires and a soul that experiences.

(((

THE SPIRITUAL JOURNEY OF OUR TIME is essentially the same journey that has occurred down through cyclical time since the termination of the Golden Age and the fall from the Paradise at the end of the primordial era. Its path commences at source within the inner self and moves outward toward the horizon of our being, then the horizon of the physical world, unto the horizon of the known universe, since it is within the self and on the horizon that we will find the essential knowledge of our meaning and final destiny. It is a human journey through time and space in search of the greatest truth for which a person is capable. Anything less than that would be mere pretence and illusion serving no purpose and leading nowhere worth going. If anything, the time has now come when we must distinguish between a purely theoretical knowledge that may only intrigue the mind and a spiritual knowledge that will transform all theoretical knowledge into a realized knowledge within our being.

Indeed the invitation to explore the inner frontier of the spirit is an unexpected challenge to our existing habits of mind and heart, requiring a new response that we may well be ready for as we now move into the new millennium. Many people today realize that they cannot continue to live in the manner to which they have become accustomed. The three gifts of consciousness, conscience and common sense are all crying out for a reassessment and change in the fundamental approach of the self to the life experience. Something has been suddenly demanded of us by the unknown frontier within and we are conscious of its persistent call to be acknowledged. Consequences could result from these newly emerging initiatives that could aid us in our transformation into the new age of our time and this will ultimately be the final journey beyond the near horizon of the self.

In more traditional times, inner worlds were more fully traveled and explored through the spiritual efforts of prayer, meditation, and any number of rites and rituals that preserved a sacred and living culture within the lives of the people. What they believed in and the manner of their thinking actually came back into the world as a well-documented and experienced narrative of man's inner life. Prophets, mystics, lamas, sages, and saints, as well as the traditional faithful down through the ages, have all explored the possibilities of the life of spirituality that is implicit within the inner life and we have their example recorded throughout history to follow. The criteria of truth has been well established within the revelation and revealed texts of the various traditional world religions. This knowledge provided more traditional peoples with a full and comprehensive worldview, explained the true nature of things, and accounted for the meaning of life with clarity and wisdom.

During these times, however, the condition of the world is bereft of the traditional perspective, leaving the spirit of the world in a state of contraction that is awaiting the possibilities of a new expansion. There are no existing maps of the inner spiritual landscape any more; nor in truth would we as modern and contemporary people desire a pre-ordained blueprint outlining the course of a new spirituality scrupulously laid out for our convenience. On the contrary, during these unique times, we must all become spiritual cartographers, examining our inner geography, plotting our own graphs, and tracing the course of our inner journey in such a way that would preclude getting any further lost than we already are. We must not lose the one thing essential to the process of living a truly spiritual life, namely faith, a supremely human faith in the Divine

Being, Who alone has the power to create and sustain everything in the universe.

Paradoxically, the twentieth century mentality seems to distinguish itself in its readiness to explore the unknown in ways that previous generations never thought possible. The fact that outer space has opened up for humanity during this century as a possibility for further exploration serves as a kind of contemporary symbol that what we are ready to accomplish on the external plane, we are also ready to accomplish on the internal plane. Indeed, space exploration is precisely what we are attempting to pursue within these pages, although admittedly we refer to the realm of inner space within the human being rather than the outer space of the cosmos. The inner human frontier presents itself as a domain worthy of exploration, a territory that is still virgin and still unexplored in terms of human potential, an area of spiritual possibility that is full of fascination and mystery, with veins of knowledge as rich as any hidden gold deposit and sources of new experience as profitable and perfect as a raw uncut diamond. We may be ready for this new expansion now, precisely because of the constricted and deteriorating era we are presently living in.

Disillusioned with the deterioration of the standards in today's world and the overall decline in the quality of life, people everywhere are developing a new sense of interest in reasonable, indeed spiritual alternatives. They are increasingly intrigued by the spiritual possibilities that have been traditionally offered to the faithful down through the ages. Individuals are becoming more aware of the fundamental mystery that lies in the human heart and within the world, and are becoming less and less intrigued with the shallow and quantified enigmas that are the specialty of the modern way of thinking. Even many members of the so-called scientific elite, perhaps because of the on-going discoveries of science, especially in the fields of biology and psychics, are beginning to reevaluate their positions *vis-à-vis* their operative understanding of the world.[9]

9. Quantum mechanics, discovered in 1927, is understood as a theory that has virtually overturned the 'traditional' scientific worldview, without replacing it most notably with a clear alternative. Wolfgang Smith's book entitled *The Quantum Enigma: Finding the Hidden Key* (Hillsdale, NY: Sophia Perennis, 2005) explores the

People are becoming more conscious of the fact that they don't have adequate answers no matter how many facts and figures they accumulate, and the answers that they do have are proving inadequate to the perennial, as well as the contemporary, needs of humanity. The unknown world of the spirit meets the unknowing world of humankind. From this encounter emerges not a field of knowledge to be conquered, but rather a vast field of exploration and discovery. Individuals are coming to realize that the unknown mystery lies within themselves first and foremost and within the outer world only secondarily and as a symbolic representation of inner, higher, and ultimately more illuminating worlds.

A final frontier still exists for mankind to explore and its wonder and mystery are not to be found in the depths of outer space. There are journeys yet to be taken through the inner space of the human consciousness that will far surpass the earthly journeys of exploration already documented. A state of spiritual wilderness continues to exist that beckons the human psyche with its mystique of adventure and its primordial holy quality. The fine line of the horizon still marks the terminus of the known world beyond which lies a mystery, a secret and a promise of fulfillment that has intrigued people down through the ages and will continue to do so as long as the image of the frontier, the sacred journey, the holy wilderness, and the distant horizon attract our interest and attention. In fact, the human mind, heart and soul—in other words the very essence of our humanity—is already situated within that frontier, ready to make a unique journey through a wilderness whose distant horizon actually suspends humanity between two worlds: the one external, visual and immediate, the other inner, spiritual and immanent.

In this way, we have come to witness the human image against the spiritual horizon of our time. We now have access to outer and

---

intricacies of quantum theory in search of a *weltanschauung* in a manner most assessable to any lay reader. 'What has happened is that the pre-quantum scientific world-view . . . has come to be disavowed 'at the top' by physicists capable of grasping the implications of quantum theory. And this in turn has called forth an abundance of conjectured alternatives, competing with one another, as it were, to fill the ontological void—a situation that has prompted one recent author to speak of a 'reality marketplace'. p1 inner worlds whose spiritual horizon marks the threshold beyond which lies the mystery, the challenge, and the promise of a unity in the reality and presence of the Supreme Being.

V

INSIDE THE
WORLD OF NATURE

And in the earth are signs for those whose faith is sure.
And in yourselves. Can you then not see?
And in the heavens is your sustenance and that
which you are promised. By the Lord of
Heaven and Earth, this is the Truth.
(51:20–23)

IN ADDITION TO the metacosmic symbol of the horizon, a nearly limitless range of traditional signs, symbols and substances,[1] both macro and microcosmic, exist within the manifested world. They confront the mind and the imagination of humanity with their revelatory knowledge of other worlds, their premonition of higher realities and their numinous message of the unity and oneness of the Supreme Being. They exist within this world as created forms that remember God through their very existence, and through their presence they express something of the transparent reality that exists within and beyond every external form. In fact, according to the traditionalist perspective, the entire created universe is a form of revelation and a sign of the Divinity. 'Thus, we live in a fabric of theophanies of which we are a part; to exist is to be a symbol; wisdom is to perceive the symbolism of things.'[2] The knowledge

---

1. By substances, we mean minerals, rock formations, precious gems, even the atom which features in the Quran as a symbolic image of the infinitely small.
2. Frithjof Schuon, *Roots of the Human Condition* (Bloomington, IN: World Wisdom Books, 1991), p 57.

and grace that make up this fabric of theophanies refer to the Divinity; existence refers to everything created in the universe; wisdom refers to humanity.

Throughout the traditional world, symbols have perennially been understood as manifested forms within the creation whose meaning conveyed none other than a spiritual reality, with a formal spiritual presence empowering the created form with its essence, thereby establishing a participation of form and spirit that was mutually inclusive as well as interactive. All the myriad forms of nature, including the orb of the sun, the crescent moon, mountains, rivers, the animal kingdom, even the atom and the gnat, speak the truth and proclaim the Divinity through their existence and their own forms of worship and praise. 'To Him belongs everything in the heavens and on earth: Even those who are in His Presence are not too proud to serve Him. Nor are they weary. They celebrate His praises night and day, not do they ever flag or intermit' (21:19–20). To be almost nothing, as in a gnat, is still something, just as to be nothing is to be almost something by virtue of the creative power of the Hand of God. Pre-modern peoples[3] understood that everything in existence had meaning; everything in existence was once a nothing made something, a God-creation *ex nihilo*. They believed that beyond every form lay a qualifying essence and that every inner essence is substantiated by the quantifying form.

The science of symbols is virtually a sacred and traditional science of sacred realities, a science of inner qualities and sacred attributes, which extends far beyond the purely physical form of the symbols inside the world of nature. Symbols do not have as their function and purpose the exposition of a graphic picture or a melodious sound. A chain of mountains or a brilliant sunset is not just a beautiful picture in and of itself. A symbol signifies the articulation

---

3. One could resort to any number of qualifying terms such as pre-modern, pre-rationalist, pre-secularist, or simply traditionalist in order to describe a mentality and an outlook that was fundamentally 'symbolist' in nature, meaning that such a mentality had a natural predisposition to understand the symbolic and therefore sacred character of all natural phenomena, and appreciated the holy and mysterious nature of the spiritual essence embedded in the natural forms within the manifested world and within revelation.

of a truth and the identification of a reality that is supra-natural and beyond the formal plane of earthly manifestation, with the suggestion of an inner world embedded within its outer form. The clarity and vividness of such symbols as the Hand of God, the Edenic Tree, and the Divine Light contain an arresting power that seizes the imagination by summarizing in an image what would otherwise be a virtual mystery, the mystery of creation, of knowledge, and of enlightenment. Sweeping deserts, vast oceans and the vaulted dome of heaven overwhelm the human mind not only with their magnitude, as in the numerical projections of modern science, but also with their power to produce meaning and induce reflection. They were never intended to be mere form, as they are understood in today's world of science. Rather, they exist as outward manifestations of the power and omnipotence of the Divinity so that humans could gain access to the inner meaning behind the phenomena of nature, thus neutralizing the tyranny of the literal form with its sacred and beatitudinal inner reality.

Symbols are a form of revelation and thus a primary source of knowledge for humanity. They exemplify in sheer form supra-rational possibilities that form the basis of understanding of the true nature of reality. They reflect multiple layers of reality for traditional peoples and relate directly to our spiritual intuition and instincts. Moreover, they are the means for the communication of a truth that would otherwise be inexpressible, a truth whose fundamental character would defy analysis because its reality is a mystery that lies beyond the range of ordinary language and beyond the power of ordinary discursive thought.

Symbols exhibit a wide range of expression from the primordial Edenic images of the snake, the apple and the tree of discriminating knowledge to the Hand (*yad*), the Light (*nur*), and the Face (*wajh*) of the Divinity. The phenomenal images of nature such as the sun, moon and stars move through the heavens and provide the setting and backdrop within the cosmic drama; but they also represent archetypal ideas that proclaim the Divinity. The unique characteristics of any given image such as the power of a rushing river, the serenity of a placid lake, the spontaneity and purity of a mountain spring, the ripples of a stream and the roar of an ocean all convey a higher level of experience that is contained within their own particularized image or sound. Every pictorial image in the creation has a qualitative aspect embedded with the graphic and often sonorous form.[4]

In other words, symbols convey a broad range of meaning extending far beyond their literal form. They are as old as the tree, as sacred as fire, as powerful as water and as mysterious as the veil. They are as enduring as marble, as beautiful as the rose, as peaceful as the dove, and as timely as the Final Hour and the Last Day. They lead beyond the surface of things and give entrance to the realms of an unseen reality. As a vehicle of knowledge, symbols are a veil, a mirror and a key. They are the protective veils of the knowledge of God, the mirrored reflection of the ideas and archetypes within higher reality, and the keys to the understanding of the fundamental mystery that underlies everything in the manifested world.

Every created thing not only exists and has meaning; but also participates in the Transcendent Principle. That is the primary meaning of the truth of the Quranic verse which states that everything in the created universe prays and praises the Divinity in a form of worship that is ontological and universal. 'Whatever is in the heavens and on the earth doth declare His praise and glory and He is the Exalted in might, the Wise' (59:24). In other words, existence itself is prayer and praise. The gnat (and other insects), the atom and the date-palm seed (and other seeds such as grain) are singled out in the Quran, the atom representing the smallest yet most powerful source of energy, the seed the basic life-giving element, the gnat the humblest living entity.

---

4. Symbols are not only visual images. They can be sounds (a mantra is a sound symbol), language (a word is an auditory symbol written down as a graphic image), a gesture, rites and rituals, sacred art, and the crafts. In other words, they can be visual, as in nature, sacred art and language; auditory as in sound, words, and music; olfactory, as in a variety of scents, including perfume and incense. Scents have traditionally been associated with a person or a presence; in Arabic, the word for smell has close derivations with such concepts as wind, presence and spirit. Jacob smelt the 'presence' of Joseph on his shirt and knew that he was still alive, although he had long since given him up for dead. In the Quran, musk in particular is named as a scent of the Paradise. Muslims traditionally apply precious oils such as musk and sandalwood before the prayer ritual; such smells have become effective olfactory symbols for the remembrance of God.

Even the lower forms of life, such as the gnat,[5] the spider,[6] and the fly[7] can serve as an example to humanity, seemingly insignificant creatures that can also convey a higher relevance and meaning. The very dust at our feet forms one of the basic elements of man's formative primordial development. 'Among His signs is this, that He created you from dust' (30:20) and unto dust, the proverbial adage reminds us, we shall return. 'When we die and become dust and bones, shall we indeed receive rewards and punishments' (37:53)? Created from dust, humans gain value by reflecting the Divine Light that shines through them, for even a speck of dust reflects a beam of sunlight upon the breast of its existence. Ultimately, on the Day of Judgment, when those who denied the truth are faced with 'that which their hands have sent forth', they will cry out the final humiliation: 'I wish I were dust' (78:40). As an end in themselves, created forms are contingent, superficial, and insignificant; as symbols of a higher reality, they are generous, eloquent and profound. All natural phenomena can be regarded from two perspectives, the physical object with a practical utility and the metaphysical symbol with its universal significance, while the symbolic aspect constitutes its most fundamental and profound reality.

Before the fall of Adam, there was no need for modes of remembrance such as symbols and narrative myths. The primordial first man was the true and universal prototype or man as an original form of perfection. The need for symbols and myths is for those who have 'forgotten' their true identity as in fallen man, not for those who instinctively 'remember' as in primordial man. Prior to

5. 'Allah does not disdain to use the similitude of things, lowest (the gnat) as well as the highest. Those who believe know that it is truth from their Lord. But those who reject faith say: 'What means Allah by this similitude?' (2:26).

6. 'The parable of those who take protectors other than Allah is that of the spider who builds itself a house; but truly, the flimsiest of houses is the spider's house' (29:41).

7. 'O men! Here is a parable set forth! Listen to it! Those on whom you call, besides Allah, cannot create (even) a fly, if they all met together for the purpose. And if the fly should snatch away anything from them, they would have no power to release it from the fly. Feeble are those who petition and those whom they petition' (22:73).

expulsion from the Garden of Eden,[8] the primordial couple, with Adam and Eve identified in revelation as the representative 'first couple', lived in a world that still retained its original perfection, a Golden Age when they 'walked with God'. They had a direct awareness of their relationship with the Divinity and they were the personification of all that the religions now try to restore for modern-day humanity. Their intuition for the knowledge of God was still integral and complete; they were still spontaneous, unassuming, and innocent; they could still perceive the transparency of all forms through a direct awareness of the forces of the spirit. They did not need a science of symbols; the symbols with which they lived every-day were living expressions of their spirit; they understood their reality to be the Transcendent Reality without the need for a symbolic veil or mirror to convey its meaning.

We can envision what this must mean by reflecting on the imperfections of our own world by way of contrast. For one thing, Adam's formal environment and the forms that surrounded him must have been far less dense and far more luminous than we could ever imagine in our existing world. In other words, there was a transparency to the formal world of primordial man that we can only imagine. When he observed his world, the Adamic man saw virtually *through* *it* to the substance of its knowledge and the inner reality that the external forms represented. The natural elements of the world around him reflected this inner spirit and this essential reality: light was a reflection of God and air was the breath of the Divine; water embodied purity and cleanliness, mountains were majesty and stability; rivers were the stream of life and its flow indicated direction and purpose. Everything in Adam's environment must have been

---

8. In itself, the garden is a momentous symbol of perfection and paradise lost towards which we all strive either consciously or unconsciously and which lies within us as an unspecified longing to return to that which we have lost at the source of our conscious experience. Adam, however, the human symbol *par excellence* of both perfection and loss, who is referred to in the traditions as the *safi Allah*, the pure one of Allah, had no knowledge presumably of the symbolic significance of the Edenic paradise. For primordial Adamic man, Eden was his natural environment; he had no need of the symbol of the paradise, for he lived its reality directly and without any veil.

transparent, not in the physical sense, but by virtue of the direct access to its inner meaning. What was outward reflected inward and what was inward reflected outward, the apparent separation between the two worlds of physics and metaphysics synthesized and resolved itself in the profound unity of the primordial world.

In understanding directly the symbolic images of his environment and as a symbol himself, primordial man was experiencing these symbols in their truest representation. The images and forms of the environment were never understood for their own sake, as we understand them today, rather they existed for the sake of the higher reality of which they were a formal manifestation. Then, the primordial test and fall from grace changed everything. The Tree of Life that Adam was forewarned to avoid proved to be too much of a temptation and at the first opportunity Adam chose the knowledge of good and evil when Satan whispered into his ear the fatal words: 'O Adam, shall I lead thee to the Tree of Eternity and to a kingdom that never decays. Consequently, they both ate of the tree, and so their nakedness appeared to them. They began to sew together, for their covering, leaves from the garden. Thus did Adam disobey his Lord and allow himself to be seduced' (20:120–121). The sacred tree of life, instead of being a direct and intuitive knowledge, became suddenly a symbol, because Adam saw the tree as an end in itself and not as a means of Divine Remembrance. In consequence, the first couple lost the direct perception of the Reality. They departed from the world of transparent forms and entered a world of symbols that would forever serve as reminders of the transparency and the spiritual reality of the Divinity as the one Reality.

Adam's legacy, symbolically speaking, is that we do not perceive the reality directly and we must now make efforts to remember the Divinity through symbols, through revelation, and through the efficacy of spiritual practices. We continue to live with the Adamic legacy of the knowledge of good and evil. We choose our path, we make efforts to remember our divine origins, and we endeavor to know through the traditional sources of knowledge, but we no longer 'walk with God'. Now we must remember the spiritual significance of forms and the sacred reality behind symbols through conscious effort rather than through the natural and spontaneous intuition that primordial man enjoyed. Now we must try to recapture the knowledge of higher realities and a sense of the sacred within the creation through spiritual practices and disciplines prescribed by all religions. Now we must raise our consciousness and express our spiritual sentiments in order to reflect the higher realities that were second nature to the primordial couple. Symbols, by virtue of their innate purpose, invite and encourage us to use those faculties that the primordial couple enjoyed naturally and that we must stimulate, including our powers of perception, our intuition of things, our natural innocence and our ability to perceive the transparency of forms. We must seek to re-instill those qualities and attributes that reflect the higher realities and that were once a direct and spontaneous reality within the primordial couple before the fall. In a word, we must rekindle the symbolist spirit within ourselves.

To that end, the Edenic Garden still exists as a reflection within the world of Nature, and the sacred sanctuaries of nature around the globe still remember the ethereal ambiance and beauty of the original, primordial garden. Adam and Eve may have fallen from grace and forfeited their direct perception of God, but the fate of the human microcosm was not the fate of the universal macrocosm. If the human being as a microcosm had lost its luminosity and primordial powers and fallen from grace, the great macrocosm that surrounds humankind, including virgin nature, the macrocosmic symbols of the sun, moon and planets, and the metacosmic spheres of space, time and the astrophysical universe that form the totality of the created universe remains intact as a symbolic image of the other side of reality. Its magnificent beauty, the harmony and order of its circular movement, its overwhelming design and perfection, and its capacity to convey profound meaning and higher emotion all point without question to a spiritual significance of the utmost importance for man.

All the elements of virgin nature still retain in principle the primordial qualities of beauty, serenity and holiness that people seek and that they can find within the sacred symbols of the world of nature if they share in the symbolist sympathy for the messages that are implicit within this natural environment. The silence of forests, the majesty of distant mountains, and the brilliance of the setting sun witness and testify to the holiness and the healing factors that are the inherent properties within nature and point to the spiritual presence that can calm disquieted minds and balance the disharmony of unhappy souls. The yearning to return to nature that we witness during these times reflects the deep-seeded yearning for the beauty, tranquility and peace that are fundamental desires of human nature, but that are far distant memories for modern individuals who must cope in their daily lives with the debilitating ugliness of the world and the stressful complexity of life in our huge, impersonal and virtually inhuman metropolises.

Nature itself is a sacred revelation and a source of knowledge, a Word, a Book and a Logos, whose spiritual meaning and significance manifests itself on many levels and through a multitude of channels. For the Red Indians of North America, their natural environment was a sacred, indeed a primordial and Edenic sanctuary through which the native tribes were able to appreciate the higher spiritual realities and realize the all-encompassing Presence of the Great Spirit (*Wakan Tanka*). For them, phenomenal nature was sacred nature because it aroused within them a sense of the sacred that permeated the entire manifested world. Forests have been considered sacred in a number of earlier traditional environments. For the Celts and the ancient Germans, the forest was the basis of their very lives and they understood the forest to serve as a kind of temple that harbored the Divine Presence, much like the Red Indians who considered all of nature to be their cathedral. In the Hindu tradition, sages and yogis retired into the forest to partake of its untouched and sacred quality. Sacred forests in India and Japan are still held in reverence by the people just as they were in pre-Christian Europe. [9] Sacred rivers and springs are another example of an aspect of virgin nature that was perennially considered to have blessed qualities. The well at Chartres and the famous spring at

9. In Lough Derg in Donegal, the most northerly county in Ireland, there is an island on which can be found a number of Christian shrines dating from the Middle Ages and also a cave, which represents the entry to the underworld. It is called St. Patrick's Purgatory for it is said that it was here that St. Patrick, the Apostle of Ireland, made hell and the Mount of Purgatory appear to the heathen in a vision. Since the Middle Ages, the island has been a place of pilgrimage.

Lourdes have come to be regarded as sacred because of the miracles associated there. The most famous spring within the Islamic world is the well known Zamzam waters adjacent to the Kaaba in Makkah, which began to gush forth, as the traditions relate, when Hagar, the wife of Abraham, was left alone with her thirsty son Ismael. To this day, the water gushes forth and services the millions of pilgrims that pass through Makkah every year. Muslims firmly believe in its sacred quality, reflecting the eternal and the immutable, and containing the blessing (*al-baraka*) that is associated with the ancient spring.

Pre-modern man, who lived in a more traditional environment than can be found today, still partook of the 'symbolist spirit' in which people were able to retain some sense of the transparency of the forms and symbols of nature, much like Adam did, and actually sensed within themselves something of the quality and attributes of the Divinity that make the human being the human image of the Divine Being. Referring to those who still enjoy the symbolist perspective of the world, Seyyed Hussein Nasr has written:

The forms of nature are for them [those with symbolist spirit] letters and words of a sacred language written by the creating power of the Divinity upon the tablet of cosmic existence. To read this cosmic book requires a special kind of literacy which is in fact very different from the literacy taught through modern education, the literacy that often causes many people to become impervious to the symbolic significance of nature and illiterate regarding the primordial message written upon the face of majestic mountains, withering autumn leaves or the shimmering waves of the sea.[10]

To read the book of Nature is to read the message of the traditional symbols that constitute the forms and elements of that Nature.

10. *The Need for a Sacred Science* (Albany, NY: SUNY Press, 1993), p122. See Chapter Eight in particular, 'The Spiritual Significance of Nature', for a complete exposé of the spiritual significance of the world of nature, especially for people living in today's world who have lost the sense of the sacred that nature proclaims through its beauty, its harmony, and its balance.

Through a willingness to partake of the symbolist spirit and through an appreciation of the value and significance of the traditional symbols in revelation and within nature, we can still have access to the original sources of knowledge that reflect higher levels of knowledge and of reality, and thus we can still know, however indirectly, 'the one thing needful.'

(((

The present age prefers the sign to the thing signified, the copy to the original, fancy to reality, the appearance to the essence, for in these days illusion only is sacred, truth profane.
(Ludwig Feuerbach)[11]

We live far from the ambiance and insight of the symbolist spirit. We live in a distant land well beyond the horizon of the traditional world in which the science of symbolism thrived and the symbolist spirit flourished. We now live in a modern world in which the symbolism of science thrives and a contemporary spirit of materialism and secularism flourishes. We pride ourselves on our creativity, imagination, and our progressive, indeed aggressive, approach to the unresolved questions that interest the modern mentality. Ancient enigmas merely await our discovery and clarification. We think of ourselves as rational beings, fully civilized, modern, scientific, progressive, secularist, and advanced in a network of treasured qualities that will lead us where we want to go. When we call ourselves civilized, we actually mean enlightened. We anticipate the answers even before we formulate the proper questions, and we express a confidence and a superiority to earlier ages that belies the underlining neurosis of our own age. We rush forward 'where angels fear to tread' and pride ourselves on our ability to reason through any enigma and solve any problem with

11. German philosopher of the 19th century, (1804–1872), taken (with author's italics) from his preface to 1843 ed. of *The Essence of Christianity* (1841), as quoted in *The Columbia Dictionary of Quotations* (New York: Columbia University Press, 1995).

our intelligence and native ability. Yet it seems that the more we learn, the less we know. The more we discover, the less we resolve. Every advance uncovers deeper mysteries and further uncertainties that generate unforeseen consequences such as over-population, pollution, and disease, psychological imbalances and rampant, senseless crime. The atom discloses the proton; the proton discloses the quantum level of energy that mockingly supersedes all known laws and overturns all theories. The facts tell us everything, yet mean nothing that makes any real sense and leave us bereft of a convincing philosophy of life.

There are no contemporary symbols to lift us out of ourselves, not in the traditional sense of the word in which an image projects onto the human plane some knowledge of a veiled reality and some aspect of an inscrutable truth that would otherwise be inaccessible to humanity. We live with a shattered atom, a replicating series of cells, the revelations of quantum mechanics, and the signature of DNA molecules. Essence is reduced to form, knowledge to information, the mind to the chemistry of brain matter, and human consciousness to the activity of neural brain waves.

Providentially, the traditional symbols still exist; we cannot do away with the sun, moon, and stars, yet we no longer see them in the same light or observe the same reflection, and we no longer read and understand their messages. The sun is a physical manifestation with mass, density and light. American astronauts have landed upon the moon and have shattered its endearing myths for all time, leaving no replacement but a human footprint now forgotten in the dusty terrain. Heaven has been diminished to mere space and its quality of eternal infinitude has been replaced with extraordinary dimensions of time and mind-boggling distances of space in the form of millions of lights years and billions of miles that have reduced the notions of infinitude and eternity to naive myths. The astronomer has lost the earth in the infinity of space, and the biologist has lost the human constitution in the infinity of time, reaching back millions and millions of years in a long progression of transitory ancestral forms that began with a replicating unicellular phylum. Perhaps it is small wonder that the drama of the crescent moon goes unobserved as it descends below the horizon of the night sky.

Who now witnesses the phases of the moon as it cuts through the night like a shining scimitar of reflected light? No one cares; we have been there and moved on. The stars twinkle their eloquent message of profound simplicity from a backcloth of infinite darkness and we no longer have the inclination or wisdom to read their mysterious message. Instead we settle for the glamour of black holes, parallel universes and the final frontier of distant space without realizing that the study of the light of the stars and galaxies we are witnessing actually represents a kind of archeology of the heavens.[12]

After centuries of philosophical, anthropological, sociological and scientific development, the conclusions we have reached from our observations of the human being and his world are: mechanism, materialism, secularism, evolution and a firm belief in progress as the ideological counterpart of evolution. In other words, we live for things and the pleasure they promise and we live for ourselves and the pleasures we experience. We reflect the mechanism implicit in the theory of evolution and we glory in the efficiency of the machine by becoming machines ourselves. We have abandoned the spiritual perspective together with the knowledge and wisdom that has shaped the mind and life of traditional people down through the ages. We blindly aspire to a philosophy of human progress and development, even though everything within the chaos and deterioration of our existing world, including the absence of morality and the sub-standard ethics of the mass population, point to a fundamental regression of the human entity. The value system that people pretend to uphold belies the myth that humanity is advancing forward, much less upward. The field of

12. Astronomers have come up with some phantasmagoric numbers concerning the distant stars and galaxies. For example, the entire universe is some 15 billion years old and roughly 26 billion light-years across, filled with stars and galaxies that are each numbered in the billions! The nearest star within our galaxy is 4 million light years away, and the most distant in *our galaxy* is 90 million light years. What this means for us is that the night sky we are observing represents a time frame millions, often billions of years earlier 'in time', since that is the time it takes for the light of those stars and galaxies to reach earth. Therefore, what we are witnessing is a galactic archeological site of immense magnitude and in no way represents the true condition of those stars at the present moment.

technology is the one area of advancement that truly astounds. Even there, however, the advancement is so spectacular and swift that the human mind still has not been able to fully accommodate its implications or develop the purpose and the *raison d'être* for these technical achievements. The primary efficacy of science lies in its technical applicability, while it remains indifferent, and in many instances antagonistic, to the spiritual aspect of reality. Instead, the primary thrust of modern science is to explain away this spiritual dimension by simply denying its existence.

I have used the collective 'we' in the previous paragraph in order to align myself with the contemporary 'we', the vast collectivity identified as the modern prototype person, for we cannot pretend to live in the modern age without being modern ourselves. Yet somehow, in spite of all the incredible technological advances in molecular biology, medical science, and genetic engineering, we maintain a superficial approach to investigating the true nature of reality. We as a civilization maintain and encourage a literal and purely analytic approach to the unknown mystery that surrounds us, together with a stubborn unwillingness to expand beyond the particularized, quantitative and exacting search for a knowledge that proposes to enrich us and make us happy. In spite of ourselves, we cannot overlook the fact that we are influenced by the modern world and are the products of this world. We live now in the 21st century, at the threshold of a new millennium; but we cannot deny the fact that the reality of our existing environment and the prevailing secular and materialistic ambiance of our world affect our bodies, our minds, our attitudes, our sentiments, our emotions, and ultimately our souls.

The meaning and spirit of the traditional world are still embodied within the symbols, the sacred imagery, the natural signs, and the manifested forms of the modern world. Yet, the traditional world itself has all but disappeared from the modern landscape. For pre-modern and more traditional cultures, certain realities transcended pure practicality and mere utilitarianism. They believed in realities that were spiritual and divine in nature, but that were reflected within this world as formal created appearances. The Greek philosophers and the Scholastics understood 'form' to be a kind of qualitative 'seal' imprinted on matter by the unique essence of a being or thing. For modern science, the essence of the form has no relevance from the point of view of its direct observation; it is not concerned with beauty or ugliness as such because it does not bear upon the understanding of its reality.

Because of the overwhelming influence of the scientific perspective on the total ambiance of contemporary life, with its accompanying by-products of secularism, materialism and rationalism, it is difficult now for people to respond to the traditional symbols that virtually surround them on all sides. Within the Islamic framework, the Muslims understand that every living thing in the created universe praises the Creator with its own *lisan al-hal*, the silent eloquence, and in particular the creatures of the animal kingdom.[13] They were created for this primary purpose. Their praise comes from being what they are and doing what they were created to do, true to their nature and in conformity to their natural intelligence and instincts. In so doing, they reflect in their actions, in their behavior, and in their very form the higher Intelligence that created them and the specific nature and qualities imparted to them by the Divinity.

All the creatures of the animal kingdom exhibit a particular quality or aspect, some higher and others lower, that highlight something unique for humanity: The determination of the tortoise, the treachery of the snake, and the contemplative resignation of the ox on the one hand; the habits (profiled in the snout) of the swine, the stink of the vulture, and the scavenging of the jackal, all exhibit an aspect of nature that are true to kind and symbolic insofar as their form is a true and honest expression that radiates a reality that is not purely physical. They are an animated representation of a prototype, picturesque in the literal sense of the word, designed to supplement the ordinary course of normal life through qualities and

13. Also for Hindus, the cow is the prototype sacred animal, and summarizes for them the concept that all living creatures are sacred in reality, symbolic and inviolate, since according to their doctrine, all consciousness participates in the Divine Spirit. The cow within the Hindu tradition is the incarnation of the maternal mercy of the cosmos. Hindus avoid injuring the cow at all cost and do not eat beef.

characteristics that emphasize aspects of a knowledge, a virtue, even a negative quality, in order to be instructive. Unlike humans, who contain within themselves all the attributes and virtues as potential qualities, animals often exhibit one characteristic that is highlighted to perfection, so that the animal becomes a symbolic prototype of a given attribute or quality.

In order to come to terms with the unseen mystery that surrounded them, traditional peoples approached all questions concerning the unknown and the unseen reality indirectly, from behind a veil, through a mirror, or by reading the signs and symbols written within revelation, within the world of nature, and within themselves. They were aware of an inner reality transcending the plane of individual experiences. In order to gain a deeper and higher level of experience, they had a broad range of symbols available to them that harbored messages of the higher realities, including the metacosmic symbols of revelation, the macrocosmic symbols of nature, and the microcosmic symbols within humans and their immediate environment. People living in a traditional culture did not consider nature in a sentimental and romantic manner as an existential mode of beauty charming to observe and pleasant to visit. For them, every natural manifestation was a reflection of a supernatural reality. By believing in and conforming to the traditional perspective embodied in the religions, they believed in the metaphysical transparency of the world. Eternity was a timeless reality brought down into the existing moment as the eternal 'now'. Infinity was the unlimited space that defined the cosmos and was brought down into our existing world through the centrality of the Infinite, a center than transcends space by being 'everywhere'.

In the pursuit of a knowledge of the purely physical and corporeal world, the modernite person has done away with the symbolic meaning of the transparent veil, the mirror of the intellect, the throne upon the waters, the river of life, the wheel of existence and all the other traditional signs and symbols reflective of an alternative reality that conveys an aspect of the Divine Mystery that could not otherwise be known. Scientists, and the rest of humanity who follow faithfully and blindly their findings, think they can approach all hypotheses and inquiries concerning the true nature of reality directly, which is tantamount to unconsciously desiring to see the Face of the Divinity without believing in the Divinity. As a result, they observe the design without the Designer, witness the implicit intelligence without recognizing the Supreme Intelligence, and wonder at the fundamental harmony within the cosmos on both the quantum and universal level without being able to affirm the Supreme Principle that is beyond its scrutiny and control.

Astronomers have put a telescope into the heavens in order to study the more distant reaches of outer space. Physicists peer through the rarefied instruments of microphysics searching beyond the level of the electron, probing within the framework of quantum mechanics for particles identified as quarks[14]. Molecular biologists, using powerfully sensitive instruments, have not only identified the well-publicized DNA chains but can also measure them![15] In the quantitative pursuit of facts and figures, a mania has developed to quantify everything in the universe, and this in turn sends the mind of the average layman into a vortex, dizzy almost to drunkenness by the sheer magnitude and infinitesimal quality of the knowledge that is being presented to him. The average layperson is unable to decipher a comprehensible meaning beyond the facts and figures presented to them, and they can formulate no understandable perspective in which to incorporate the knowledge that is being 'discovered'. Astronomers tell us that the universe is approximately 15 billion years old, that there are billions of stars in a galaxy and indeed billions of galaxies. The sheer numbers are overwhelming, but the information itself is somehow burdensome and lacks any

14. Quarks, whimsically identified as up, down, charm, strange, top (or truth), and bottom (or beauty) are elementary particles that make the subatomic power we have thus far named look immense by being immeasurably smaller than the electron even.

15. In the case of bacteria, whose dimensions are measured in 1/1,000 of a millimeter, DNA forms a tape whose length is measured in millimeters. In the case of man, for one single cell, the DNA tape is long enough to be counted in meters. The total length of DNA tape contained in a human being is greater than the distance that separates the earth from the sun (P. Kourilsky), cf. Dr. Maurice Bucaille's *What is the Origin of Man?* (Kuala Lumpur: A.S. Noordeen, 1982) where he gives an in-depth expose of the origins of life from both the scientific and traditional point of view, based on Quranic sources.

kind of explanatory power. Distances within space are quantified and measured in light years: The nearest galaxy (the Andromeda nebula) is 2 millions light years away. A spaceship would arrive there after a journey of 2 million years traveling at the speed of light, yet we refer to these things as if they were the neighbors across the street! The most distant galaxies are as far as 10 billion light years away and to astronomers these distances are nothing if not numbers to stand in awe of. To the average person, they mean nothing.

The stream of facts is curiously unsatisfying because such detail lacks a qualitative meaning that we can incorporate into our being. Without the perspective of the Infinite and without the implications of the Eternal, we are left adrift, with the human mind floating literally in a cosmic space bereft of meaning. The facts simply paralyze the mind and benumb all feeling for the unexplored universe; they do not translate into meaning because they have no symbolic significance from the scientific point of view. The true value of the stellar world lies in its pictographic projection of a boundless universe in harmony with the laws of a Supreme Being, and this is reflected in the symbolism of its profound holiness, its extraordinary magnitude, and its unfathomable mystery. Its ultimate value most notably does not lie within rational formulations of its material structure and measurable limitability, but in its ability to convey a meaning of profound and unspoken omnipotence through the dark canopy of its symbolic projection. Outer space symbolically represents the realm of the Eternal and the Infinite. It is the sole environment that can adequately reflect the living Presence of the One Reality.

It is not enough to know *that* something exists; we must know *why* it exists. The purpose of existence reflects meaning, while the facts of existence and their literal face, though interesting and informative, reflect a cerebral human curiosity to quantify the truth for utilitarian purposes alone rather than benefit from truth's universal significance. Meaning must lie at the heart of existence, meaning for humanity, for the world, for the cosmos. Symbols provide that meaning at every level of existence from the atom to the vast galaxies of the universe. We do not need to know that the universe spans umpteen miles and billions of light years in diameter if knowing this data cannot be converted into a knowledge that enlightens and a wisdom that saves.

A revealing feature of the modern world is the fact that the 'collective psyche' of modern individuals, to use a Jungian[16] term, no longer recognizes the symbolic nature of the world and has replaced the symbolist spirit of the traditional person with a literal-minded and slavish approach to the true nature of reality that denies the mystery of the supra-rational realities. The modern mentality is no longer capable of seeing the celestial Cause in the terrestrial effect because we have lost the means to penetrate into the inner meaning of phenomena that organic nature reveals through its symbolic imagery. By thinking that we can approach truth directly, we have altered the very meaning of truth in ways we are only beginning to realize. We cannot approach truth directly any more than we can see the Face of God. Moses heard the voice of God from behind a burning bush; the Prophet Mohammed received the words of God through an intermediary, the Archangel Gabriel; but they and the other Biblical and Quranic prophets did not see God. In wanting to see the face the Truth directly; modern sophisticates wish to see the Face of God on their own terms.

Perhaps we should let the scientific facts speak for themselves on

16. Jung has come to be known as the 'father' of modern psychology. He is responsible for coining such terms as the 'collective psyche' and the 'collective unconscious' which he describes as a 'common substratum' of the psyche, and he includes them in the 'collective knowledge' of humanity. Regrettably, perhaps unconsciously, he is also partially responsible, much like Darwin with regard to evolutionism, for disturbing the traditional view of humanity concerning the purpose and meaning of symbols. See C. G. Jung, *The Secret of the Golden Flower* (New York, 1931), where he writes in his introduction: 'The fact that this collective unconscious exists is simply the psychic expression of the identity of cerebral structures beyond all racial differences... the different lines of psychic evolution start out from one and the same trunk, whose roots plunge through all the ages. It is here that the psychic parallel with the animal is situated.' Further on, he adds: 'It is this that explains the analogy, indeed the identity of mythological motives and of symbols as means of human communication in general.' Thus, Jung confidently links the traditional myths and symbols with some kind of inner psychic fund that further identifies and associates the human being with the animals, similar to the theory of evolution. Jung never attempted to mold the basis of his psychology within the traditional framework of the mind (intellect) and the heart (spirit) of man.

their own level while allowing truth to be what it is. Let the facts accumulate according to the human capacity to scrutinize and analyze them, and let the symbols serve in their capacity to reflect and to synthesize, serving as signposts of the Way and as shadows of the hidden Source of Light. Let the facts speak for the truth as long as they don't deny the truth or change its meaning into something unrecognizable and false. The key is not in the pursuit of knowledge for its own sake or for the sake of the curiosity of humanity; the key lies in the pursuit of a meaning that transcends the literal forms of the creation. Knowledge as an end in itself is the worst form of heresy. It is the only true heresy that exists in a pure form because it refuses *a priori* to accept a truth that is beyond the control of the human mind. It limits our capacity to think and belittles our nature. It denies that we are more than animals and affirms much less. Knowledge as an end in itself inhibits the increase of human knowledge, human wisdom, human reverence, human achievement, and the human awareness of God. It cramps the soul and the spirit and declares that all things are nothing but constituent matter. It proclaims that nothing is sentient, especially not the human mind. It worships the mammon of stone and not that which the stone represents, namely the existence of God, His Oneness, and His Visage.

The traditional forms, in the manner of signs, symbols and the sacred substances of the earth, still exist. We behold them every day of our lives. They cannot be destroyed, in spite of the efforts of those who endeavor to destroy the symbolist spirit of earlier cultures in order to cultivate the secularist ambiance that prevails today. The traditional signs and symbols continue to guarantee the knowledge of God in their reflection and they continue to ensure the flow of divine beneficence in the form of celestial *baraka* or grace. They transcend anything that is in the power of humanity to produce, for they are the virtualities of the Infinite.

Similarly, for those people who still believe in the transcendent reality at the heart of all existence, everything is relevant and nothing is impossible because the universe is inscribed with the signature of the Divine Being. Flowers, incense, and perfume contain a scent that reflects presence; a cloud contains rain which brings mercy and blessing; even the symbol of wine, mentioned in the Quran as a provision of the Paradise, is holy nectar that elevates the spirit without intoxicating the mind. Everything has a sacred essence embedded within the physical form, and the majesty of the Divinity is reflected in all things. His shadow lies within the mountains; the face of Heaven sweeps across the waters; His heralds soar through the skies; His legions roam the earth. His Origin resides in the smallest bud; His voice thunders through the valleys. The world teems with the effulgence of God; nevertheless we as representatives of the modern ambiance see only the form of a thing and neglect its sacred meaning and holy remembrance.

If present and future generations could perceive the inner substance and spirit beyond the outer shell and molecular constitution of forms, then nothing would be an absolute problem for them. If they held firm to their faith in the revealed nature of reality, they could conquer, not the world, but themselves. The very forms of the manifested world, through their revelatory symbolism, would help them achieve their end, namely fulfilment, transcendence and union with the Divine. Nothing can come between the spirit of humanity and the Spirit of God except a closed mind and a misguided will. Every divinely created form is a symbol of a higher reality, and the realization of this lies in the truth that all the phenomena of nature proclaim the Divinity and prove it by the miracle of their existence.

VI

READING THE MESSAGE OF NATURAL SYMBOLS

The earth is full of signs in evidence of the work of Allah.
They are perceived by those who are certain of the truth.
(51:20)

IN LIGHT OF the symbolist spirit of the traditional world, perhaps the moment has arrived to rekindle this spirit within the modern, indeed the post-modern environment as a means of integrating the phenomena within nature with an intuitive understanding of the higher realities that the natural order reflects. Perhaps it is time to refresh our memories and recall the latent forces of perception that exist within the human mind. It is again time to read the messages that abound within the created universe. It is time to remember that we still have the capacity to observe and understand the inner messages that are conveyed to us through the sacred symbols and substances within the natural order. It is time once again to open our eyes, to release the forces of our inner psyche, to activate the broad reasoning powers of the human mind, and to draw upon our spiritual intuition in order to understand the sacred knowledge that lies within the symbolic forms existent in the creation. It is time to liberate the well of sacred emotions within the heart that has traditionally been considered the 'seat' of the intelligence as well as the source of all sacred sentiment. It is time to make ready the ground of our souls, in order to raise our consciousness and activate a living awareness of the principial truth. We need to realize once again and remember that the truth, the reality and the spirit that we seek clothes itself within our world as manifested forms that represent a universal confluence of the creation. As such, symbols come to our aid and eloquently express something meaningful about the hidden reality that hovers below the surface of the manifested world like a promise awaiting fulfillment.

Because of the generosity and spirit of the Quran available to Muslims today in its original and unaltered form, the Muslim mentality[1] still remains steeped in awareness of the value and significance of traditional symbols, and it still has preserved something of the symbolist spirit that traditional peoples instinctively exhibited. One reason for this lies in the fact that the Quran, taken in its totality, is the most direct symbol of the spiritual world, both in its totality and in its multiple fragments of letters, words and sounds, all of which constitute a 'sacred science' of symbolism in Islam. In addition to its implicit symbolic value, the Quran repeatedly entreats the faithful to observe the signs (*ayat*) that are everywhere visible. 'It is He Who has sent among the unlettered a messenger from among themselves, to rehearse to them His Signs, to sanctify them, and to instruct them in Scripture and Wisdom' (62:2).

Muslims have traditionally been deeply interested in the relationship between the outward manifestation of the world, the origin of the human entity, and the reality of the Divine Being. For Muslims, everything serves as a sign and symbol of God. Nature is the macrocosmic revelation and the human being is the microcosmic revelation. On both levels of manifestation, a Muslim has the opportunity of acquiring knowledge of God and of the true nature of Reality if they recognize the signs that are available both on the horizon, within the natural order and above all on the near horizon within themselves. Everything is significant and meaningful within the

---

1. We refer to the Muslim mentality as we might refer to the traditional or the modern mentality. Certain characteristics and features of mind stand out within the majority of the Islamic community, the collective Islamic *ummah*, traits such as hospitality, charity, and a kind of resigned detachment that accompanies belief in a God of absolute power whose Mercy, according to a well known Holy Tradition, precedes His Wrath. Certainly, the universal acceptance of the symbolic nature of the universe within the Islamic community also aptly characterizes the Muslim mentality as symbolist.

creation; nothing is insignificant and subject only to random and chance occurrence. 'Everything We have created and prescribed for it its measure, its character and destiny (54:49). No creature creeps on earth but Allah provides for it its sustenance. He knows its purpose and destiny. For it is He Who prescribed them in His eternal order' (11:6).

As microcosmic symbol of a higher reality, nearly every aspect of the human body serves as a specific symbol[2] with a particular mandate that ultimately leads back to the Divinity. For example, the heart (*qalb*) and breast (*sadr*) of the human body are mentioned repeatedly in the Quran. The *sadr*, the inner chest and heart cavity, has traditionally been associated with the act of surrender to the Divinity which in Islam is the initiation into the religion and the very meaning of the word *islam*. 'Is one whose heart [*sadr*] is open to Islam, so that he has received enlightenment from Allah [no better than one hard-hearted]' (39:22)? On a literal level, the *sadr* or breast is the encasement of the lungs, but on a figurative level, it recalls the expansion and contraction, the aspiration and expiration, of the human spirit. The human breast as the sacred chamber of expansion and contraction recalls the names of God, the Expander (*al-Basit*) and the Contractor (*al-Qabidh*) as the source of the human spirit.

The heart (*qalb*), on the other hand, has traditionally been considered the 'seat' of the intelligence[3] and the repository of a person's faith (*iman*). 'Allah has endeared faith to you, and has made it beautiful in your hearts, and he has made hateful to you unbelief, wickedness and rebellion' (49:7). The heart combines the knowledge of God together with the spiritual emotions, both of which interact in order to create the longing for the Divinity and the certitude that accompanies a man's faith. Within the inner chamber of the heart

2. 'Have We not created for men their eyes, their tongues and lips? Have we not granted them their senses of orientation' (90:8–10)?

3. This may come as a surprise to the modern mentality that associates all intelligence with the cerebral mind. Intelligence in the traditional view is not mind but rather an interaction of mind, intellect, and heart and is directly associated with the knowledge of God. To be intelligent is to know God; to be wise is to act upon that knowledge.

lies the *fu'ad*, or inner heart, and this is activated for high ranking Prophets and saints (*awliya*) who are able to apprehend and experience the intuitive knowledge of spiritual truth. The heart is also the seat of the *ma'rifa*, or the intuitive, gnostic knowledge that the Holy Prophet Mohammed received from Allah (53:11) together with another person, unidentified in the Quran[4] but referred to only as 'one of Our servants, on whom We had bestowed mercy from ourselves and whom We had taught knowledge from Our own presence' (18:65).

The human heart is not the only organ mentioned in the Quran that has symbolic value and properties that extend far beyond its physical image and function within the corporeal system. The eyes, nose, ears, mouth and hands are all instruments of the senses as well as symbolic images that lead to an inward knowledge. Space and thematic constraints do not permit us to elaborate too extensively concerning specific symbols and their related meanings. The Quran itself stands as the eternal reference to the sights, sounds, images and symbols that reflect the higher realities. It is enough perhaps to make mention of the fact that virtually every major aspect of the human body, from the fingertips to the feet, is mentioned symbolically in the Quran in order to suggest a meaning or a specific emotion relating to the content of the symbol. The jugular vein is well remembered because of its proximity to the life force and more importantly because the Divine Being has said: 'We are nearer to him than (his) jugular vein' (50:16). The heart itself is referred to innumerable times in multiple verses and different contexts: hearts are open (39:22), locked (47:24), and sealed (30:59 et. al.). Hearts sigh and express regret (3:156); others are filled with disgust and horror (39:45). They whisper (114:5) and they repent (64:4). Some hearts are deceased (47:29; 2:10), other hearts conceal what they know (40:19). Some unfortunate hearts rise up into the

---

4. The traditions suggest that this refers to Khidr, who knowledge was 'special' since it came directly from the Presence. Khidr is a mysterious being who was sought out because allegedly he had the secrets for the paradoxes of life which ordinary people do not understand. St. Paul writes about him in one of his epistles to the Hebrews (v. 6–10; vii. 1–10): 'He was without father, without mother, without descent, having neither beginning of days nor end of life.'

throat (40:18). Finally, hearts are referred to as strengthened in faith (58:22), devoted (50:33), and pure[5] (*salim*) (37:84). Ultimately, the heart 'finds satisfaction in the remembrance of Allah, for without doubt in the remembrance of Allah do hearts find satisfaction' (13:28).

The Hand of God is a universally accepted symbol of power, creativity, skill, and sensitivity. The human hand expresses all these attributes by way of reflection; it does not mean on some literal level that God has a hand. Concerning the Divinity, the Quran tells us that 'In Your Hand is all goodness' (3:26) and 'the Hand of Allah is over their hands' (48:10). In addition, hands are the symbol for deeds accomplished (78:40). While bounty lies in the hand (3:73), hands are also used to kill (5:28), destroy (59:2) and bring misfortune (42:30). Ultimately, human hands have earned what they have done (30:41) and will send forth (30:36) in front of them that which they have accomplished in this life in order to be weighed on the scales of justice.

Two symbolic images that feature highly in the Quran and that are embedded within the mind, heart, soul and thus the mentality of every Muslim are the image of the home and the image of the way. The image of the home has been immortalized in the well known Arabic expression *dar-as-salaam*, the home of peace. The concept of home has traditionally been associated with both origins and final ends and inevitably summons feelings of safety, security, familiarity and comfort. In addition to the *dar as salaam*, or the home of peace, the Quran refers to the home in the hereafter (28:77). This is none other than the final abode and it is described as the home that will endure (35:35), the eternal home (41:28), and the permanent home (40:39). Finally, there is also the home of misery (40:52); those who dwell there will not be able to escape.

The symbol of the way is none other than the familiar straight path (*sirat al-mustaqeem*) mentioned in the opening *sura* of the Quran and repeated by the Muslims during the recitation of the

---

5. Most notably, Abraham is identified as having a heart that was pure (*saleem*) and unaffected by the diseases that afflict others. Abraham is called *Haneef*, the True One (2:135).

prayers. 'And unto Allah leads straight the Way, but there are ways that turn aside' (16:9). The Quran mentions a number of different roads, paths and by-ways in order to emphasize the concept of the journey of return that the faithful are embarked upon, a journey that will ultimately bring them to their origin and source in union with the Divinity. We have already mentioned the narrow *sirat* or 'bridge' spanning across the flames of hell that, according to the tradition, everyone must cross before entering the Paradise. During prayer, Muslims entreat the Divinity to guide them on the straight path, and the Quran itself has come down as the truth 'that guides to the path of the Exalted (in might), Worthy of all praise' (34:6). There are two highways that humans have been shown on the earth; one is the steep and difficult path of virtue, and the other is the easy path of vice and the rejection of God, 'but he hath made no haste on the path that is steep' (90:10). In addition, the Muslims are encouraged to follow the middle course (35:32) and the path of righteousness (40:10). The earth is described as a carpet with roads (43:10) through which the faithful may find guidance. The Quran advises the faithful to follow the middle course (35:32), even though man is inclined to follow divergent paths (72:11). Some people take the path that is identified as the *sabeil Allah* (61:4) or the causeway of Allah (His way and His cause combined into a single image); others take the way to the fire (*sirat al-jaheem* [37:23]).

In terms of symbolic imagery, perhaps we are most familiar with the images of eschatology catalogued with graphic clarity in the Quran. These include the scales, which will be set up so that 'not a soul will be dealt with unjustly in the least even if there be (no more than) the weight of a mustard seed' (21:47), the balance which is a universally understood symbol of justice and equilibrium, and the bridge between worlds. The bridge suggests the dangerously narrow passage that leads over the fire into the sublimity of the Paradise. The Quran refers indirectly to this bridge in *sura* 19, verse 71, when it states 'not one of you but will pass over it', in referring to those who are 'most worthy of being burned' in the fire. In addition, there is the familiar eschatological instrumentalia most directly represented by the searing fire that burns but doesn't consume, the boiling oil, the revolting drinks and the putrid smells that will assail the damned. These are well known and should be understood not in their literal sense but in the fundamental spiritual reality behind the symbol that suggests a just recompense for one's actions.

Certain individuals and objects are associated with the prophets and serve as identifying symbols. Jacob's ladder immediately comes to mind within the Biblical context, but the Quran abounds with references to particular and specified objects or even members of families that Muslims immediate associate with any number of messengers and prophets. Adam, of course, is mentioned as the first man,[6] the one tested, the one fallen; yet he is still referred to in the traditions as *safi Allah*, the pure one of God. Sacrifice is always associated with Abraham and the son of Abraham always calls to mind implicit and unwavering faith, in counterpoint to the father of Abraham (6:76) who represents infidelity and faithlessness. Hagar, the wife of Abraham and the mother of Ismael, is well remembered for her stamina and endurance during her frantic search for water between the Makkan hills of Safa and Marwa. The wife of Pharaoh,[7] (66: 11) represents the triumph of faith, humility and righteousness over faithlessness, arrogance and injustice. The wife of Zachary (*Zachariah*) represents a triumph of another kind, when he cried to his Lord: 'How shall I have a son, seeing I am very old and my wife is barren? 'Thus,' was the answer, 'Allah accomplishes what He wills' (3:40). The wife of Zachary reminds us that nothing is impossible with the Divinity; we are His instruments and vehicles; their son, the Prophet Yahya, proves this. The wife of Noah and the wife of Lot are also specifically mentioned in the Quran as powerful human symbols of rejection and faithlessness. They are both identified with the wicked worlds Noah and Lot departed from and left behind.

Similarly, certain objects associated with the prophets have symbolic value. Muslims remember the white hand of Moses, shining as with a divine light. The Quran also speaks of the foot of Job (38:42),

6. Eve is not directly mentioned in the Quran by name.
7. Traditionally known as Asiyah, she is considered one of the four perfect women, the other three being Mary, the mother of Jesus, Khadijah, the wife of the Holy Prophet, and Fatimah, his daughter. Asiyah is thought to be the same woman who saved the life of the infant Moses. (28: 9)

the sandals of Moses (20:12), the strength of David (38:17), who could make iron soft and pliable (34:10), and his gift of music (38:18), for David is the prophet who wrote the Psalms which are considered to be some of the most beautiful of the Biblical verses. The Quranic revelation specifically mentions the wind and staff of Solomon (34:12) as well as the mirrored floors of his palace. Jacob is remembered for his patience ("patience is beautiful against that which you [Joseph's brothers] assert' [12:18]). Joseph himself is remembered for his shirt, firstly because it was smeared by his brothers with false blood, secondly his shirt ripped from behind proved his innocence against the advances of the noblewoman of the Pharaonic court, and thirdly his scented shirt signaled for Jacob the presence of his beloved son Joseph. Zachariah is remembered for his silence,[8] Yahya is remembered for the Book that he held fast to.[9] Jesus came to humanity as an incarnation of the word (4:171) and he was a sign (43:61) and a messenger for the people, both then and now.

Traditional symbols have the power of remembrance embedded within the sacred form of the human body even, symbols that can trigger within the human mind a sacred memory of the Divinity and a spiritual experience of the highest order. The human senses participate in the language of symbols. For example, the sense of taste features highly in the Quranic terminology.[10] Humanity will eventually 'taste' a broad range of experiences that range from sublime rewards to loathsome punishments. It is repeatedly mentioned that the believers will taste the blessing and mercy of the Divinity (30:46). The unbelievers, on the other hand, shall taste 'a boiling fluid, and a fluid dark, murky and intensely cold' (38:57). Above all, believers and unbelievers alike will taste the fruits of their deeds,

8. 'He said: "O my Lord? Give me a sign?" "Thy sign," was the answer, "shall be that thou shalt speak to no man for three days but with signals."' (3:41).

9. '(To his [Zachariah's son came the command); "O Yahya! Take hold of the Book with might"; and We gave him wisdom even as a youth' (19:12).

10. The Sufi, or Islamic mystics, have traditionally referred to the experience of dhawq, which literally means 'taste' but has come in higher religious circles to mean the experience of the Divine through a taste of knowledge, an intuition, and thus an experience.

tasting in some cases humiliation (39:26), eternal punishment (32:14), and the corruption they have earned (30:41). Ultimately, 'every soul shall have a taste of death' (3:185) as the final earthly experience and in a world of doubt the ultimate certitude.

Human minds witness and have faith. Human wills surrender and act upon their beliefs. The human face is set steadily and with true piety in the direction of the pure religion (10:105). The five senses will all bear witness, including the eyes for what they see, the ears for what they hear, the mouth for what it says, and the skins for what they feel (41:20). Bellies will be filled with the fruit of a tree 'that springs out of the bottom of the Hellfire, the shoots of its fruit-stalks are like the heads of devils' (37:65). Yokes will be put on the necks of the unbelievers (34:33) 'up to their chins so that their heads are forced up (and they cannot see)' (36:8).[11] The knee is the focus of kneeling and prostration (45:28), while in the traditions the beard has been called the 'light of God'. In addition, there is a 'sign' in the variety of colors [races] (30:22) and in the multitude of languages (tongues). The image of the tongue is the universal symbol for language, the mother tongue being one's native and original language. The Quran itself has been delivered in the 'tongue' of the Arabs (44:58). The twist of the tongue can become an instrument of slander (4:46). The tongue of the prophets David and Jesus pronounced curses on those who had disobeyed and persisted in committing excesses among the children of Israel (5:78).

Similarly, the revelation refers to the hypocrites as those 'who say with their lips what was not in their hearts' (3:167) and those of the unbelievers 'who say 'We believe' with their lips but whose hearts have no faith' (5:41). The mouth can be the instrument of enmity and evil. In speaking of those who corrupt others, the revelation says 'They desire only your ruin: rank hatred has already appeared from their mouths: What their hearts conceal is far worse' (3:118). *Homo sapiens* is actually powerless in the shadow of the Divinity and this is no more fittingly symbolized than through the human forelock, which is as it were the crown of beauty that Allah has

11. The wife of Abu Lahab will have a twisted rope of palm leaf fiber around her neck (111:5).

firmly in his grasp (11:56) like a trainer with his horse. Sinners, who
are well known by their 'marks', will be seized by their forelocks and
their feet and dragged into hell (55:41). The skins of those in the
hellfire will roast and 'as often as their skins are roasted through, We
shall change them for fresh skins that they may taste the penalty'
(4:56). On the other hand, the 'skins of those who fear their Lord
tremble; then their skins and their hearts do soften to the celebra-
tion of Allah's praises' (39:23). Stomachs will be filled with the fruit
of the Tree of Zaqqum, which is identified in the Quran (17:60) as a
cursed tree; while the bowels of the unbelievers will be cut into
pieces by a disgusting drink of boiling water (47:15). Fingers are
thrust into ears by those who want to block out the knowledge of
the true reality (71:7) or they will bite off the very tips of their fingers in their rage (3:119). Feet are mentioned many times throughout the revelation, for they are traditionally the symbol of firmness,
stability, and deep-rootedness, all aspects that are usually associated
with a strong spiritual determination and a sincere faith. Feet are
actually referred to as firmly planted (47:7) for those who follow the
cause, the way, the *sabeil* of Allah, while the believers will only ask
their Lord to forgive them their transgressions and establish their
feet firmly on the ground (3:147). Finally, in a symbolic picture of
the agony of death, the soul will reach to the collarbone (in its exit)
(75:26) as it takes its reluctant leave from the body.

In addition to the anthropomorphic symbols, there is also a
geometry of symbolization that is significant, meaningful and
immediately recognizable. The dot, as already mentioned concerning the diacritical point under the Arabic letter *ba*, has traditionally
been conducive to visualizing the transcendent center. It is the primordial and absolute point, source and final end, first drop of the
Cosmic Pen and end point of the cosmic narrative. It summarizes
both the microscopic and macrocosmic realms within a center that
remembers core, heart, kernel and ultimately the ever-mysterious
essence. The line emerges out of the primordial point, commencing
all movement, direction and destination. The straight line is none
other than the straight path of scripture, the most direct avenue
between two points. The crooked line moves off the mark and represents in a single image all that is errant and devious. The inner

line of every individual reflects purpose and intent; to follow one's inner line is to remember the Divinity. The absolute point becomes the infinite circle, a circle that remember the circle of evil (48:6) as well as the circle of knowledge, in which the Divinity encompasses all.

Finally, there is the geometric symbol of the hourglass. The visual image of the circle merges by extension into the cycle of life and of time and this is rendered most fittingly through the symbolic geometry of the hourglass whose peculiar shape has come to mean termination, finality and the certitude of death as a prelude to resurrection, renewal, and transcendence. No unbeliever will enter the Paradise unless the proverbial camel passes through the 'eye' of the needle; but every living thing will pass through the hourglass. Its inverted semi-circles converge at its isthmus or eye, through which flow irreversibly the sands of time. Concerning the created universe, the image of the progression of time is but an hour, a day, or a fragment of eternity that is measured through time. Concerning the Divinity, 'Our Command is but a single (act), like the twinkling of an eye' (54:50).

(((

TRADITIONAL SYMBOLS can be characterized primarily by their beauty and their efficacy. Firstly, let us consider the symbol in terms of the significance of its essential beauty.

For one thing, the symbol can be called beautiful by virtue of its actually being what it gives expression to and represents, namely a spiritual truth and a higher reality that is reflected within the form. 'A symbol is not something arbitrarily chosen by man to illustrate a higher reality; it does so precisely because it is rooted in that reality, which has projected it, like a shadow or a reflection, onto the plane of earth.'[12] In other words, we say that a symbol is beautiful primarily

12. Martin Lings, *The Eleventh Hour: The Spiritual Crisis of the Modern World in the Light of Tradition and Prophecy* (Cambridge, England: Quinta Essentia, 1987), p36.

because it is true. The beauty of an object results from the transparency of its form through which a truth is made known, and there is nothing more beautiful than a truth that is made manifest in a particular form. Secondly, a symbol can be called beautiful because it has a universal character and says something of the Unity that lies at the heart of the universe and is its mirror reflection. 'The beauty of a thing is the sign of its internal unity, its conformity with an indivisible essence, and thus with a reality that will not let itself be counted or measured.'[13]

A machine[14], for example, is not beautiful, although it is the conventional symbol *par excellence* for the modern world, full of utility and efficiency, but totally lacking in the subtlety, grace and truth traditionally associated with beauty. It may be efficient, functional, utilitarian, economical, and technologically advanced, to name its most obvious qualities; but it does not reflect a truth or identify a spiritual reality. A swan[15], on the other hand, incarnates within its very form an aspect of dignity that is virtually archetypal. By isolating this formal aspect of perfection within an animal, it makes the animal not only beautiful but also symbolic of a higher spiritual quality. There is an entire range of animals that actually projects direct and immediate impressions of a symbolic nature. These animals highlight for mankind one of the higher qualities or otherworldly attributes toward which we aspire, the intrinsic beauty of a symbol lying in its meaning and in its truth rather than in its form *per se*.

The lamb and the dove, in addition to the swan, are animals that project a quality of innocence and a feeling of peace that borders on the otherworldly, while their white color remembers the celestial purity. The owl projects wisdom through its physicality and 'image',

13. Titus Burckhardt, *Mirror of the Intellect* (Albany, NY: SUNY Press, 1987), p33.

14. It could be argued that a machine is a symbol, because it is a form that represents an idea concerning means and end that is realized with precision if not with grace. A traditional symbol is not an earthly form created for merely a pragmatic and utilitarian end; rather it is a formal means to a spiritual end.

15. In the Hindus tradition, the divine swan Hamsa, swimming on the primordial sea, hatches the golden egg of the world.

without having the wherewithal to actually be wise. The bear manifests an aspect of heaviness and cunning, and it literally retreats into
the earth (cave) for its winter hibernation. The squirrel, on the
other hand, elfin and almost cherubic in appearance, shrewdly
gathers and stores its nuts for the winter, and remembers where
they are when it needs them. Who can look upon the astute activity
of the squirrel and not wish to incorporate this proverbial quality
into themselves? The camel suggests patience and contemplation,
not to forget its ascetic aspect that is curiously reflective of the harsh
environment of the desert where the camel thrives. The bee[16] is an
'inspired' animal that produces honey through its 'instinctive' intelligence and whose skill in house building reflects the divine wisdom. The ant,[17] a lowly creature indeed, was honored by Solomon.
The ant, among other social insects, has been a source for all kinds
of parables, giving lessons in industry, interdependence, altruism,
frugality, humility, patience and endurance. All of these animals
reflect at least one of the higher qualities towards which humans
aspire and, in endeavoring to exist through the instinctive animal
intelligence granted by God, they express their individual symbolic
qualities to perfection, without corruption or compromise.

In addition to the engaging symbolism of the animal kingdom,
the symbols of nature are stunningly beautiful and virtually define
the meaning of beauty. Anyone who has witnessed the drama of a
sunset, the enchanting quality of the night sky, or the artistry of a
snow crystal knows what the beauty of nature can be and is. Yet,
how is it possible to further articulate this beauty in words when the
symbols themselves serve this purpose so magnificently? The quality of nature's beauty and truth is reflected firstly in its sense of

16. And thy Lord taught the bee to build its cells in hills, on trees, and in habitations; then to eat of all the produce of the earth, and find with skill the spacious
paths of its Lord. There issues from within their bodies a drink of varying colors
wherein is a healing for me: verily in this is a sign for those who give thought' (16:
68). Most notably, the entire Sura 16 of the Quran is named al-Nahl, the bee.

17. 'At length, when they came to a (lowly) valley of ants, one of the ants said:
"O yea ants, get into your habitations, lest Solomon and his hosts crush you (under
foot) without knowing it"' (27:18). The entire Sura 27 of the Quran is named al-
Naml, the Ants.

order and harmony, which by implication conveys to humanity a feeling of certitude that behind this order and intelligent design lies a supreme Mind that is reflective of a Divinity who has created these awesome phenomena. To participate in the world of nature creates a sense of peace that leads to tranquility of mind and serenity of heart.

In addition, nature conveys the unmistakable impression of sacredness and primordiality. That is why it always produces a spiritual experience that borders on instinctive worship of the Unseen Reality by conveying the feeling that, through the open face of nature, we have witnessed indirectly the clear Face of God. The grandeur of the primeval forest, the majesty of the open seas, the magnitude of the heavens, and the sublime wonder of the night sky all induce higher levels of awareness through such spiritually emotive experience, the reason being that these symbols all reflect higher levels of reality and indeed the Divine Being Himself who has created that reality. As such, all of nature, what we refer to endearingly as Mother Nature, transcends the normal modes of symbolic expression because Nature is actually beautiful beyond words and beyond belief.

Consider, for example, the elements and substances of nature, how they have developed and grown within certain optimal conditions that were conducive to their order and design. Is this pattern of development an accident, a chance happening, some form of necessity as many modern scientists would have us believe, or are we dealing once again with the miracle of the creation symbolized by the Hand of God. We only need to think of the great substances of nature such as diamonds, gold, silver and other natural elements, how beautiful and desirable they have always been. Think of the qualities of such precious stones as the transparent crystallinity of diamonds, the bold color of emeralds, sapphires and rubies, the perfection of pearls, and the solidity and smoothness of marble. Even the varieties of wood that characterize certain trees make statements that extend far beyond the literal constitution of the tree. We are thinking here, for example, of the majesty of the oak, the dignity (and scent) of pine, the verticality of the poplar, and the ethereality of the willow. All these objects within nature are natural and pure, without artifice or pretense. They express integrity and completeness, and they speak a message to all those who appreciate these natural images and substances, a message expressed most eloquently through the voice of silence. Precious stones in particular are known to have a unique resonance whose sympathetic vibration can have a soothing, even healing effect on a person. Ivory has traditionally been used for carving exquisite statuettes and other handicrafts because of its unusual color and pliability; while marble has provided the source material for ancient monuments and world renowned sculptures because of the implicit beauty of its configuration, its integrity of stone, and its simplicity and purity. Wood has traditionally been associated with the sense of smell or taste. Pine is remembered for its exquisitely odoriferous scent evoking the mysterious lure of the woodland forest; frankincense is the weeping sap of a tree found in the Sultanate of Oman. Vermont maple syrup is an edible sap drawn from the inner seams of the maple tree.

(((

ULTIMATELY, the beauty of a traditional symbol lies in its efficacy, and this is essentially threefold. The symbol is simple, it is universal, and providentially it is true.

Like all spiritual knowledge and its corresponding wisdom, the symbol is first of all simple, yet profound. For those sensitive to their intuitive message, the traditional symbol moves from the outer world of humanity to the interior plane of human consciousness with immediate impact. Its simple, clear image appeals first to the eye with its incarnate image and its veiled meaning. Its picturesque impression then moves quickly inward from eye to mind to heart to soul. It imprints itself on the retina before opening and expanding the mind to the substantive meaning of the symbol. Beyond eye and mind, the message of the symbol proceeds inward to the heart wherein spiritual sensibility and intuition come into play in order to transform the literal meaning of the symbol, whether it be an image, a word, a sound, a gesture, or a sacred rite, into an irresistible and intuitive impression of the Higher Reality and the Divine Source whose remembrance takes root in the ground of the human soul.

Because of their fundamental simplicity and directness of projection, symbols help clarify the mystery of the world. Admittedly, we are perennially in doubt about our origins, our purpose on earth, and our ultimate end. In addition, we are forced to acknowledge the truth of an all-pervasive mystery that lies at the core of manifested existence and defies all logical explanation. The profound simplicity and directness of symbols clarifies—through an image, a gesture, a word, or a sound—an idea or an aspect of knowledge that would otherwise be inaccessible. They have the power to summarize and condense within form the very essence of a meaning that may otherwise elude our intellectual grasp, particularly in this day and age when we think with our minds rather than with our hearts, unlike the people of more traditional times, for whom the heart was the virtual 'seat' of the intelligence.

The symbol is not a rational definition; as such, it does not suffer the limitations that purely rational thinking exhibits. Symbols are pictorial and descriptive, not theoretic and argumentative. They are affirmations rather than theories and convey a graphic meaning by way of illustration through pictures, gestures, or words, and not through rational arguments and sensory proofs. Definitions and meanings that are the result of a purely rational mind organize concepts according to their logical and purely rational implications, but they do not leave an open door to an extended reality beyond the limitations of the mind. The symbol, on the other hand, while it does not lose any of its precision or directness, remains openly 'vertical' and is a key to the supra-rational realities that would otherwise be beyond our conceptual and cognitive reach. The symbol is neither rational nor irrational, as some might suggest; rather it is supra-rational and vertical.

Moreover, the simplicity of the symbol embodies a profundity of meaning. Its image contains an extraordinary power to summarize within an understandable frame of reference a profound mystery. It has the power to call to mind the archetypes that correspond to ideas and intellections that lie beyond the human plane. Archetypes belong to the realm of pure spirit and are reflected on the psychic plane as virtualities of deeper truths that eventually become crystallized as actual images in the real world. They provide a graphic and distinctive explanation for the human mentality of a reality that must remain veiled from direct view. In this way, the vast majority of humanity can gain access to spiritual insights concerning the mysteries and the true nature of reality as long as individuals are open and receptive to the natural symbols that abound in the world of nature. It is as if an understanding of the value of the science of symbols and its corresponding symbolic language opens the door to an unexpected but welcome insight. If you could effectively read the message of symbols, would this give access to the totality of the truth that lay behind these earthly images? If you understood the principial knowledge behind the semblance of symbols, would the wisdom of all other subjects become apparent as well? If you could know in your inner being one thing fully, could you, in a manner of speaking, know everything?

Even universal questions require individual answers; that is why individual symbols have universal meaning. Beyond their beauty, efficacy and simplicity, symbols project a quality of universality that complements their quality of profound simplicity. They are not bound to any individual religion; that is why they are referred to as traditional and not religious. When people are moved by a symbolic image, gesture, word or sound, they don't think they have something to do with religion; they think they have something to do with truth, reality, and the spirit, all of which transcend the individual forms of the religions. The picturesque and symbolic image of the mountains has always called to mind 'the heights' and the proximity to Heaven. Perhaps that is why mountain climbers have always attempted to scale their peaks, often without fully knowing why. People have looked toward and climbed mountains throughout the ages because they represented the abode of the gods. To climb a mountain was to approach the Heights and the Presence.

The image of the heavens has always presented an immediate image of the cosmic universe and its seven heavens have always conjured up the idea of the multiple layers of reality that are manifested both within and beyond the human plane. The Divine Throne prevalent within the Christian and Islamic traditions summons to mind the cosmic power, authority and dominion of the Divinity, as the well known Throne Verse in the Quran attests: 'His Throne doth extend over the heavens and the earth' (2:255). The sun universally exhibits centrality and luminosity. Among the various traditions, it represents the Universal Intellect, while the moon has traditionally been associated with the beauty of the beloved because of its pale, reflective light. The sacred Tree of Life is a concept that goes back to ancient times, rooted to the earth but reaching for the heavens. It features in both the Christian and Islamic traditions as the pivotal image of knowledge and life. Adam was tempted with the Tree of Eternal Life and because of his fatal choice it became for him the Tree of Knowledge between Good and Evil.

One of the greatest symbols of all time, widely recognized because of its comprehensiveness and universality is the symbol of the veil which, as *maya* in Hinduism and as *al-hijab* in Islam, plays an important role in Middle-Eastern as well as in Oriental metaphysics. Humanity is veiled from the immediate and direct perception of the spiritual realities through a formal and manifested world that is in itself a veil. This veil is increasingly opaque during this time period because the modern mentality exhibits a narrow understanding of reality as embodied within the framework of modern science, a science that refuses to recognize the transparency of the world and settles instead for the literal interpretation of the world as a reality unto itself.

The veil has been traditionally understood as being two-edged in its meaning and implications. On the one hand, the veil acts as a solid barrier to further insight in which no penetration into the true nature of reality is possible, such as we find during these times. The veil of knowledge protects itself from the uninitiated, the unwilling, and the unfaithful. On the other hand, the veil also serves as an open door, such as we find in the science of symbolism and within the symbolist spirit, and becomes transparent so that a human intuition and an appreciation for the higher realities can become possible for the human mentality that is willing to lift the veil. Thus, the veil of knowledge within the traditional framework both protects and reveals, and the veil of the world both hides and manifests the true nature of reality.[18] In Islam, one of the Holy Traditions states: 'God has seventy thousand veils of light and darkness; were He to draw their curtain, then would the splendors of His Face (*wajh*) surely consume everyone who apprehended Him with his sight.' Also, the archangel Gabriel has said: 'Between me and Him are seventy thousand veils of light.' In the ancient Egyptian traditions, no one shall lift the veil of Isis. Isis is 'all that has been, all that is and all that shall be;' and 'no one hath ever lifted my veil.'

Water is the Great Purifier of body and soul, the universal symbol of purity and purification. For the Hindus, the waters of life find their embodiment in the River Ganges, whose source resides in the eternal ice of the Himalayas, the mountains of the gods and the roof of the world. Whoever bathes in the Ganges is freed from all sins. Water also symbolizes the *materia prima* of the whole universe. In the Bible, the Spirit of God moved upon the face of the waters, while the Quran reconfirms this truth with the words 'and His Throne was over the waters' (11:7). In addition, Quranic scripture asserts that 'We have made from water every living thing' (21:30) and 'He sends down water from the skies, and the channels flow, each according to its measure' (13:17). Everything in nature speaks the truth, proclaims the Divinity, and reflects the inner reality through the expression of natural forms. All the miracles that the eye perceives within the natural order begin as a mystery of creation and ends as a proof of God.

One final example may serve to highlight the broad nature and universality of the traditional symbols. We refer to the well-known symbol of the mirror that has been referred to as 'the symbol of the

18. 'In a symbol there is concealment and yet revelation: here therefore, by silence and by speech acting together, comes a double significance.... In the symbol proper, what we can call a symbol, there is ever, more or less distinctly and directly, some embodiment and revelation of the Infinite; the Infinite is made to blend itself with the Finite, to stand visible, and as it were, attainable there. By symbols, accordingly, is man guided and commanded, made happy, made wretched.' Thomas Carlyle, a Scottish essayist of the 19th century, in his *Sator Resartus*, bk. 3, chap. 3, as quoted in *The Columbia Dictionary of Quotations* (New York: Columbia University Press, 1995).

symbol'.[19] Symbolism generally provides an ambiance that creates within our daily lives a symbolic link with the transcendent and unconditional Reality of which our relative reality is but a reflection. Symbols provide a visible and graphic reflection of ideas and archetypes that cannot adequately be expressed in words. St. Paul summarized it succinctly in this well known quote from the New Testament: 'For now we see through a glass, darkly; but then face to face: now I know in part; but then shall I know even as also I am known.' (Cor. 13:12) Within the Buddhist tradition, a teaching from *Ch'an* Buddhism concerning the implications of the mirror states: 'Just as it is in the nature of a mirror to shine, so all beings at their origin possess spiritual illumination. When, however, passions obscure the mirror, it becomes covered over, as if with dust.' (*Tsung-mi*). Within the Islamic perspective, according to a saying of the Prophet Mohammed, there is 'for everything a means of polishing it and freeing it from rust. One thing alone polishes the heart, namely the remembrance of God' (*dhikr Allah*). The world, and those who live in that world, are both a veil and a mirror, veil through sheer physical form that conceals the truth from direct perception, and mirror that transcends the physical form through its symbolic projection in order to reflect the truth of the one Reality. The universe as macrocosmic mirror is the universal body of God, just as humanity as microcosm is the human 'image' of God and as mirror reflects God's qualities and attributes.

One final attribute of the traditional symbol and perhaps its most striking characteristic needs mentioning, in addition to its beauty and its universality. A symbol is ultimately true because it represents a truth. It brings a veiled reality of the Divine Mystery down into the world of humanity in order to make it a living reality through images, symbols, signs, and substances of the natural and visible world. The essence of their truth and their immediate reality formalizes the objective reality that they remember and reaffirm. Above all, the truth implicit in symbols still has the power of transforming the modern mind, whose scientific worldview perceives the

19. Titus Burckhardt, *The Mirror of the Intellect* (Albany, NY: SUNY Press, 1987), p118.

reality in all the density of its physical projection, into a symbolist spirit whose vision perceives the world as a reflection and remembrance of the Higher Reality.

By attempting to lift the veil that separates the known world from the unseen reality, the faithful can empower themselves to become their own symbol and thus their own revelation. By reading the inner message of symbols, they can reflect the qualities and attributes of their Creator who is both Reality and Truth (*al-Haqq*). By witnessing the world of forms as symbols of a higher reality and as mirrors of a higher knowledge, people today can once again witness eternity in time, the absolute in the relative, spirit in form, and thus transform the temporal shapes of natural phenomena into the timeless symbols of a universal reality.

PART C

THE HUMAN IMAGE OF GOD

Traditional people understand themselves to be a veil and a key, veil because they do not instinctively know themselves and key because like all traditional symbols, the knowledge of God lies sequestered within their beings as the resolution to the perennial mystery. Just as nature is considered a revelatory book of knowledge, Homo sapiens *is considered the human revelation and a living source of knowledge. This knowledge identifies humans as spiritual beings capable of knowing The Transcendent Being and thus capable of internalizing that knowledge within the ground of the soul as the fundamental truth of their existence.*

VII

THE SYMBOLIC
IMAGE OF MAN

HUMAN REVELATION AND
LIVING SOURCE OF KNOWLEDGE

He who knows others is wise;
He who knows himself is enlightened.
(Tao Te Ching, XXXIII)

When Ali asked Mohammed: 'What am I to do that I may not
waste my time?' The Prophet answered, 'Learn to know thyself.'
('Aziz ibn Mohammed al-Nasafi)

WITHIN THE TRADITIONAL WORLD, the power of the symbol lay
in the meaning it could convey, a meaning needless to say that could
not contradict truth without betraying its own *raison d'etre*, a
meaning that in being truthful to its image would remember and
reflect the Divine Spirit who is the origin of all form and thus the
source of all meaning. As such, the world and the universe that
encompasses it are majestic symbols of a Supreme and Transcendent Being who is the Creator of the universe. All the manifestations of the creation, from the innumerable symbols of nature here
on earth to the vast cosmic setting that serves as a universal backdrop to that world, constitute a synthesis of symbols that have the
power to make an impression spontaneously and directly that
affects the mind and the being of all humans.

The image of human beings as a prototype entity, stripped of all the information we know about them as a biological and historical reality, forever remains a powerful symbol of the Highest Reality. Whether this human prototype is identified as primordial man, traditional man, or the modernite individual of today, they still embody the essential elements that permit them to transcend the world of form and the earthly horizon. Indeed, according to all the revelations of the major world religions, *Homo sapiens* is the living prototype of spirit within form, constituting physical flesh and blood and bone that has been raised to the level of an intelligent, thinking and self-conscious being, a soul and thus a spirit, who in reflecting the Spirit of God becomes the living symbol *par excellence* and a human revelation in microcosm of the knowledge of God. Like Revelation and Nature, human beings are considered a primary source of knowledge, the final of three primary sources of traditional knowledge still available to humankind.

The world of the spirit that is reflected in the traditional world seems to have been absorbed by the spirit of this world, if we can refer to the predominantly secular ambiance of this world with the word 'spirit', for there is not much in the way of a traditional spirit within today's world, a spirit that above all remembers the Spirit of God within humanity, within the world and within the universe as the sublime projection of the Universal Self. This does not mean that the spirit is not there within all created forms or that symbols are no longer symbols. But the divine disclosure of God through the Word, through Nature and through Man no longer serves the needs of humanity as in more traditional times, for the simple reason that we no longer recognize these three points of reference as the primary and valid sources of essential knowledge. People today continue to rely on the power of human reason and the professed objectivity of physical matter to verify the truthfulness of ultimate reality, indeed *the* Reality. Through these two arbitrary norms that are firmly established within the consciousness of man today,[1] these

---

1. A consciousness it is worth pointing out that modern man self-confessedly cannot begin to fathom unless modern scientists can convincingly trace its origins and source of 'prescience' to the molecules and 'gray matter' of the brain.

two reference points constitute the main source of knowledge in today's post modern world in the quest for knowledge of a unified reality that conforms to the laws of science.

The traditional sources affirm that while the ultimate Reality is one, the earthly reality[2] is two, constituting a fundamental duality that not only characterizes but also defines the nature of the universe. Within the Quranic terms found in Islam, there is the powerful traditional image of the isthmus (*barzakh*), a well-known symbol of the duality of this world on the one hand and the polarity of 'this world' and the 'otherworldly' on the other hand. These two worlds identify and form the two fundamental domains within the creation of an exclusive, rarefied, and unified Reality. The Quran makes reference to the isthmus between the two seas, the one distinguished by its pleasant sweetness and the other by its bitter saltiness. Like the horizon, the two seas separate two worlds and/or two degrees of reality, and like the horizon, they also unite these two worlds through symbolic projection by virtue of the fact that the two seas meet, joined together by the isthmus that forms the bridge between worlds.[3] 'He created the two seas that meet together, between them an isthmus they do not overpass' (25: 53). As bridge, the isthmus unites alien worlds in the same way that the neck of the hour glass and the figurative meaning of the natural symbols do, bringing together through image and symbol the seemingly disparate worlds of matter and spirit, thus unifying the two half-truths into a single, unified reality.

(((

MUCH HAS BEEN MADE during these times of the image of the modern human prototype as a figurehead of evolutionary growth and progress reflected through linear time, a being who commenced at some point in the past whose ancestral lines goes back to

2. I write 'earthly reality' because this is how we as human being perceive our immediate reality to be, since we are 'of the earth'.

3. As such, the isthmus exists also within the heart of man, since man is also an isthmus between worlds, a meeting point and a bridge.

the origin of life and whose progress entails the transmigration across multiple species in a grand march of evolutionary continuity that finally comes to rest in the future of itself as a post modern person. It does not seem to matter exactly what that image entails in terms of meaningful projection or whether those images of development reflect anything significant beyond the sheer evolutionary hypothesis in the image we have become. We are told by modern-day scientists, for example, that 'life' as distinguished from 'dead matter' made its spontaneous emergence as a living possibility from self replicating molecules embedded in organic clay crystals that commenced this grand evolutionary march, ultimately reaching its pinnacle in *Homo sapiens* who has the prescience (and temerity) of mind to question the likelihood of such an origin and provide answers that are supposed to make sense.

In addition, paleontologists have observed sufficient data from fossil, bone and skull evidence to speculate that the inquisitive simians of antiquity emerged from the trees of their traditional forest home because of a cooling climate, whereupon they roamed the great African Savannah in search of food and ultimately a way of life best suited to their changing needs. Gradually, the great apes came to stand and move on two legs, to make and use stone tools and weapons, to reduce the size of their canine teeth and to enlarge the size of their brains—only God knows how—for the biology, the chemistry and the physics involved in these processes are never explained by paleontologists beyond the invocation of the scientific rationale of natural selection whose native insight and wisdom match that of the gods of antiquity. Anatomical considerations have led modern science to believe in a profound ancestral link with the great apes by virtue of the similarities of our bodies, in terms of both physical image as well as their proximity in biology and chemistry.

Furthermore, because self-consciousness and a thinking intelligence reflected uniquely through spoken language seems to be two of the identifying marks of our humanness, scientists are forced to identify the 'cognitive efflorescence', to quote the inventive words of a paleontologist, that eventually generated the high level of spoken language and conscious awareness displayed by *Homo sapiens*. As such, paleontologists envision three stages in human history: the origin of bi-pedalism, the origin of the big brain, and the origin of introspective consciousness. Our 'humanness', indeed humanity itself, is questioned and speculated upon in theoretical terms by legions of scientists in any number of scientific fields, without being able to identify not only a credible origin for a 'human' person, but also without being able to articulate a convincing meaning for such an entity in the first place, as if modern scientists, in failing to identify the defining quality of the human person, does not have any idea of the true identity of the human being they are investigating and hoping to come to terms with. The genuine and often notable successes of modern scientists in describing *Homo sapiens* lies in their ability to articulate only the nature of the corporeal form in terms of its biology, chemistry and physics.

Under the circumstances, then, what if anything can we learn from the outer shell about the inner person, for who a person is must reside in some realm beyond the physical form surely? Any inquiry into how we identify ourselves must commence with an understanding of who we are in our totality and where we find the origin and source of our life and consciousness, a perennial question that only the spiritual traditions through revelation and indirectly through nature have managed throughout the millennia to adequately resolve? Modern science has made tremendous strides in uncovering the mysteries of the human body, including the chemical and biological intricacies of human growth and development; yet, because much of the evidence of human origin and development comes from fragments of anatomy, enigmatic archeological assemblages, and DNA gels in molecular biology laboratories, the question of the meaning of humanity and how they identify themselves remains quixotically unresolved even today, perhaps especially today in light of the loss of the spiritual perspective and the traditional way of life that once supported the more eclectic traditional perspective. A philosophy of science has evolved over the years and exists, but it amounts to a philosophy of denial of the traditional paradigm of knowledge based on an assemblage of facts that offers no credible alternative.

It is not enough for scientists to deal with the issue of human origins on the purely physical level of expression, reducing the image of the human being to a well-defined pictogram rather than the symbol and synthesis of the Divine Being that he/she really is according to revelation. The existence of modern humans forces scientists to think about human existence as an individual, formal species. Yet surprisingly, among scientists today, there is not even an established definition of the quality of humanness. Our defining humanness seems to defy the logic of pure scientific reasoning by virtue of its abstract quality if not its insistent and living presence, bringing about a groping for explanations for things that they know instinctively exist and that everyone has experienced, such as emotions and qualities of being, but that don't fit within the established frame of reference of reason and physical matter.

The noted paleontologist Richard Leakey, in attempting to come to terms with the mandate of paleontology, writes:

> Because the target of the search is ourselves, the enterprise takes on a dimension absent from other sciences. It is in a sense extra-scientific, more philosophical and metaphysical, and it addresses questions that arise from our need to understand the nature of humanity and our place in the world.[4]

At least, he attempts to put the dilemma confronting modern science within a working perspective that includes other dimensions of experience beyond the purely scientific one. Yet, when it comes to defining ourselves and identifying what sets us apart from the rest of the animal kingdom, modern scientists convey the impression that we are groping in the dark. To quote Leakey once again with reference to human origins, he writes despairingly:

> If all of this appears to be a confusing and uncertain picture of modern human origins, it is precisely because anthropologists and archeologists themselves are not yet sure what actually happened. Much as we should like to know the answers to this major period in our history [specifically the time period involving the

---

4. Richard Leakey, *Origins Reconsidered: In Search of What Makes Us Human* (New York: Doubleday, 1992), p xvi.

decline and death of the Neanderthals], we are certain only of the questions.[5]

Nevertheless, the modern scientific view of humanity turns from the present day back into the antediluvian past when the world was populated, not by *Homo sapiens*, but by the great apes, the pre-human hominids, and the enigmatic anthropoids, whose unholy evolutionary narrative shapes the very image and identity that we see of ourselves. Indeed, if we actually believe that an ancestral line passes us back physically through the hominids to a formal simian ancestry, what does this mean for the origins of our mental, emotional, psychic, and spiritual condition and the dramatic narrative of their development? Can we be expected to believe that these inner elements of our human constitution find their origin and source in a great ape, and if so, from whence do they derive their elemental power and force, much less their very presence? Are we to believe that the autobiography of man is written on the skull visages of intermediary beings and in the strata of rock formations?

The mental capacity of human beings has evolved and increased, so that the intellectual, technical and creative minds of people today seem to belong to another species than that of rural peasants with their slow reactions and dull, methodical manner. Human impulses, however, in the form of feelings, emotions and desires—the counterparts of our thought processes and our knowledge—do not seem to match the tremendous advances the thinking person has made over time. Collectively, we know more during this age than at any time in recorded history, and yet our fundamental impulses, our behavior, our perceptions of right and wrong and our consciousness of ourselves and the world around us have remained almost changeless while the entire world has been transformed over the ages.

This century alone has witnesses the development of electricity, the telephone, the splitting of the atom, the venturing into space, the identification of DNA and other biological wonders, technological advances such as the computer and the Internet all of which dazzle the mind and thrill the intelligence with their virtual possibilities

5. Ibid., p235.

and unlimited promise. That accounts perhaps for what we can *do*; but not alas for who we *are*. Someday our brains will finally catch up with our instruments, the wisdom of our behavior may match the knowledge of our brains, and our purpose in living may match our powers of accomplishment. Then, perhaps, we may have advanced and made 'progress' in the spiritual as well as the material sense; then, at last, we might behave like true human beings.

There is a strange disparity between the sciences of inert matter and the science, in the traditional sense, of man. Astronomy, physics, and their related sub-groups are based on concepts that can be expressed tersely and elegantly in the language of mathematics. Modern scientists have built up a universe as mysterious and grand as the monuments of ancient Greece. They weave about their theories a magnificent texture of calculations and experimentation in order to 'prove' their theories and hypotheses. They search for a theory of a unified reality beyond the realm of common thought and beyond the reach of common man. The universe has become for us a magic forest that can be transformed into whatever we want it to be in our imagination and in pursuit of our theoretical speculations. Yet, we have come no nearer to understanding the universe of man, either his true identity or his ultimate purpose, than we have come to understand the great macrocosmic universe beyond man. In the traditional world, the human being was the greatest of earthly symbols. In today's world, the human being is a image without a symbolic meaning, modeled upon a vague and humanistic image, rather than as a thinking person created *in the image of God* (Gen. 1:27).

Our ignorance of ourselves is profound. Most of the questions put by those who study human beings today remain without convincing answers, whether they concern man's mysterious origin on earth or his ultimate meaning and purpose. Even on the purely physical level, immense regions of our inner world are still unknown. How do the molecules of chemical substances associate to form the complex and temporary organs of the cell? How do the genes in the nucleus of a fertilized ovum determine the characteristics of the individual deriving from that ovum? How do cells organize themselves by their own efforts into tissues and organs? Where do the cells derive their intelligent design, not to mention the very intelligence that drives them? Like the ant and the bee, the cells seem to have advance knowledge of the part they are destined to play in the life of their community. We know that we are a patchwork quilt of cells, tissues, organs, fluids, and even consciousness; but the relationship between consciousness and cerebrum is still a mystery.

The science of inert matter has made immense progress over the course of time and particularly during this century, while the knowledge of living beings remains in a rudimentary state with regard to the conditions of human existence, the intricacy of the phenomena of life, and the form and manifestation of our intelligence and emotions. The applications of modern scientific discoveries have transformed the materiel and even mental worlds into fields of experimentation and have exerted on us a profound influence. This unfortunate result stems from the fact that they have been made without consideration for our true nature. The environment born of our intelligence and our investigations is adjusted neither to our stature as human beings nor to our inner nature.

Just as the astronomer has lost the earth in the infinity of space, the biologist has lost the human person in the infinity of time resulting in the long and discontinuous progression of transitory species that find their pinnacle in the confusion and uncertainty of today's world with the human species on the brink of an unknown future in a new millennium. Our ignorance of the totality of ourselves has given to biology, physics, and chemistry the power to modify at random the ancestral forms of life, and yet innerly we remain the same, or perhaps worse, we degenerate morally and spiritually in spite of ourselves and in spite of the fact that our overdeveloped and super-charged minds cannot process or integrate the higher realities that make life possible in the first place. The science of matter takes precedence over the knowledge of humanity, and this places us within the precarious position of knowing everything about the world of matter and nothing about the world of man.

The macrocosm that has been created by astronomers and physicists, and the microcosm created by chemists and biologists have no universal basis and do not conform to the reality of humanity or the universe. Despite the stupendous magnitude of the physical cosmos and the subtle intricacy of the genetic and cellular worlds within man, in the final analysis, the world of matter does not satisfy us on fundamental levels. It does not move us innerly because it has no hold over our minds or our souls. Indeed, not only the average person but also scientists themselves cannot understand the significance and implications of much of their theoretical findings. For this reason alone, we cannot adhere to a faith in its exclusive reality. We know that we do not fit within its purely physical dimensions. We still know on some deeper, instinctive level that we extend somewhere else, outside of and beyond the physical continuum.

Man is a corporeal body and thus a physical object, but he is also a living presence and a focus of mental, psychic and spiritual activity. His presence in the prodigious void of inter-sidereal space is totally negligible and without consequence in today's ambiance of rationalism and materialism. Admittedly, it is true that we are not a stranger in the realms of physical and inanimate matter. With the aid of mathematical abstractions, our mind apprehends the electrons as well as the stars. We are made of the same material as the mountains, oceans, and rivers and we live within their scale. We belong upon the surface of the earth, exactly as trees, plants and animals do and we feel at ease in their company. However, we also belong to another world: a world that exists within as a microcosm and that is reflected within the world of the macrocosm. We live and breathe a conscious reality that begins within as a living consciousness of self with a life of its own and that stretches across the universe beyond the horizon of space and time through the consciousness of the Metacosmic Reality.

In our mental, psychological and spiritual development, we must now move on. We must liberate ourselves from the myopic vision of modern science and the tempting lure of high technology and seize the wealth and potential of our own nature. The sciences of life have shown to humanity their goal and placed at its disposal the means of reaching it. We are still immersed in the world created by the sciences of inert matter; but we need not remain entrenched within a paradigm of knowledge and a worldview that is born of an error of our reason and thrives through the illusory impressions of our senses. It is a worldview that is made *by us* but nor *for us* because it does not respect the laws of our spiritual dimension and does not recognize the truth of our spiritual inheritance. Postmodern humanity must become less mechanical and more human; they must become less cognitive and more receptive. They must use their intelligence more intelligently and their innate free will more freely and willingly, with creativity, imagination and sensitivity of heart. As we move hesitatingly into the 21st century and the new millennium, the complete person may well become the new frontier of knowledge and science, and not the fragmented person that exists today.

(((

IN SPITE OF THE EXTENSIVE RESEARCH done in a variety of scientific fields, including biology and chemistry, on defining human origins, constitution, evolution, the workings of the intelligence, the psychology of the mind, and ultimately the true nature of human consciousness, modern science still cannot define humanity. The perennial question concerning our true nature and identity basically remains more of a mystery today than it has ever been down through history. For all of the answers that modern science has uncovered concerning the physical constitution and make up of human beings, major gaps still exist in our knowledge of self that strike at the core of our self-consciousness. Is the human being the symbolic image of the first Adamic man who originated as a perfected being and then passed through phases of fallen, traditional, and modern man searching for fulfilment and perfection that is the legacy of his primordial being. Or are we the result of blind and random forces that have been shaped through the guiding hand of natural selection and has led to the unlikely result of a 21st century thinking person?

According to the Quran, God asked the human soul at the dawn of creation: 'Am I not your Lord?' Man's definitive answer 'Yes, we witness You' (7:172) resolves the fundamental question that lies within the heart of every human being: Who am I and how do I identify myself? This human affirmation pours the soul into a mold of surrender and faith that permits a person to acknowledge the truth of the Divine Being as the One Reality. This affirmation of soul places the human being on an inward track of self discovery in which the question of one's true identity becomes rooted in the knowledge of God and the answer becomes the means to realize that knowledge. The question becomes the knowledge of a way of life and the answer becomes the wisdom of a life well lived.

For the traditional person, the Divine Being identified Himself in revelation through ninety-nine qualifying names and attributes in order to make accessible His supreme identity to humanity. Similarly, we can identify ourselves by becoming the human expression of the qualities and attributes of God in order to make our identity known to ourselves and to the God who created us. By virtue of this interaction between the Divine and the human, we also becomes in principle a synthesis of knowledge waiting to be known and a theophany capable of worship and intimacy with the Divinity because we are a reflection in human terms of the divine attributes and qualities.

Traditional peoples understood themselves to be both a veil and a key, 'veil' because they do not instinctively know themselves as primordial, Adamic man did and 'key' because like all traditional symbols, the knowledge of God lies sequestered within as the practical answer to the perennial and universal question of human identity. Just as the world of nature is considered a revelatory book of knowledge, so also is the human being a human revelation and living source of knowledge. The symbols of the veil and the key form the basis of a sacred psychology that identify both the human mystery in view of the mystery of the Absolute and the existential challenge to realize one's full potential on earth through worship and effort. Humans are a veil unto themselves in which they must lift the barrier that exists between their own conscious, externalized self and their supra-conscious, inner core. Because of human intellect and the power of free will, they are not only a veil but also a key, capable of unlocking the psychological and spiritual forces that rest within the human mind, psyche and soul that need to be utilized if we wish to fulfil ourselves. This sacred human psychology results in our being identified as spiritual beings capable of acknowledging the Transcendent Being. Humanity is thus capable of internalizing that knowledge within the ground of their souls and has it available as the need to use it arises over the course of life.

To say 'human' recreates in a word the subjectivity of man. To say 'being' recreates in a word the objectivity of God within humanity. Thus, 'human beings' find themselves the expression of a duality in search of a unity, much as we suggested earlier that people today understand themselves to be a question in search of an answer. Humans cannot be a purely objective being in and of themselves. If they were, what would be the basis of that objectivity and the lodestone of such aspiration? Nor can they be a purely subjective being, for then they would have no ground in which to take root and grow. Martin Lings puts his finger on the pulse of the problem:

> There is not one of us who is not aware of powers within which are at an incomparably higher level than anything outward and visible. They could be summed up as our subjectivity and our objectivity, our subjective consciousness of being 'I', which is inextricably bound up with the mystery of life, and our objective intelligence, which is capable of grasping truths that infinitely transcend our empirical experience.[6]

We cannot deny the reality of our 'other self' without giving up the totality of who we are.

No one would deny that truth runs through the human entity like an invisible thread, but many people may seriously doubt that it ties humanity irrevocably to a Universal Reality (al-haqq) both unifying and unique. To misunderstand the nature of truth and the compelling reasons to acknowledge its existence as an all-embracing reality is to forfeit the knowledge of God. To want anything less than the truth and its implications is virtually to want the wrong thing. Every person today, as in the more traditional times, needs to include within his or her perception of reality that which is not within the grasp of the physical senses only. The true journey is inward toward a process of spirituality and upward toward a state of consciousness and awareness in which God is infinitely close to humanity,[7] both as a

6. *The Eleventh Hour: The Spiritual Crisis of the Modern World in the Light of Tradition and Prophecy* (Cambridge, England: Quinta Essentia, 1987), p 40.

7. The Quran emphasizes this point through a vividly clear image of the unimaginable proximity of God to man. 'We are nearer to him than his jugular vein' (50:16), and on a more intimate level, another verse proclaims: 'God comes in

spiritual reality and as an existential experience. This is made possible for no other reason than the fact that the human being possesses a human consciousness that manifests initially as a subjectivity and an individualized soul whose spirit remembers and reflects the objectivity of God that lies secreted within the human heart.

Needless to say, from the spiritual point of view, the modern individual has a serious problem. Because people have lost the direct knowledge of God through their failure to acknowledge and value not only revelation but also its theoretical possibility, they have also lost the direct—indeed the revelatory—knowledge within themselves that must be the necessary by-product of the knowledge of God. Each of the world religions has emphasized this point concerning the knowledge of self as prerequisite and prelude to the knowledge of God.[8] If the well-known tradition (*hadith*) of the Prophet be true, namely that 'He who knows himself knows his Lord,' so also must it be true that if we have lost our knowledge of God then we have also lost our capacity to truly understand ourselves.

Without the totality of the knowledge of God, whose name in Islam is also the All-Encompassing (*al-Wasi*), we must rely on knowledge—not *of* ourselves which is in keeping with the concept of the self-revelation of man, but knowledge—*by* ourselves and on our own, with a virtual dependence on the externalized, indirect knowledge that we is able to gather by virtue of human reason and through the accumulated data of the senses. However, while the knowledge of the senses may be immediate and poignant from the point of view of earthly experience, this knowledge is also superficial from the spiritual point of view, a knowledge of the surface only or merely surface impressions without accounting for the totality of reality. As S. H. Nasr has succinctly put it: 'Fragmented knowledge

---

between man and his own heart' (8: 24). Man separates himself from God, but God is never fully separated from man, unless he is damned which means definitive and unalterable separation from God.

8. 'He who knows himself is enlightened.' (Tao Te Ching) 'Thou believest thyself to be nothing, and yet it is in thee that the world resides.' (Avicenna) 'Let me know myself, Lord, and I shall know thee.' (St. Augustine) 'Oh that we would but once learn to know ourselves!' (Boehme) 'The being is all that it knows.' (Aristotle)

can be related to the whole only when there is already an intellectual vision of the whole.'[9]

The human being was intended to embrace the truth in its totality and not settle for half-truths that mislead him along the path or outright falsehoods that turn him away from the path.

> The modern psychological and psychoanalytical point of view tries to reduce all the higher elements of man's being to the level of the psyche, and moreover to reduce the psyche itself to nothing more than that which can be studied through modern psychological and psychoanalytical methods.[10]

Thus, post modern individuals living today, who find their identity within the ground of their own being, is reduced to a place mid-way between a half-truth and an absolute ignorance, making themselves a human lie and a false god at the same time.

Above all, the spiritual perspective provides a comprehensive view of humanity and the world that is fully understandable to the traditional peoples provided that they apply its underlying principles to the existential facts of his existence. Unlike modern psychology, traditional sacred psychology does not rely on quantitative analysis of the human being, but rather relies on the qualitative dimension of an essential knowledge that comes down as revelation from a Divine Being, a knowledge that has the power to synthesize and unify humans at the core of their being, as a unity, as a center and as a synthesis, in reflection of the unity at the center of the Divine Being. As a result, the revelation of God meets the human revelation in the mystery of self knowing, in the manner of their being, and in the manner of their becoming known.

9. S. H. Nasr, *Islam and the Plight of Modern Man* (London: Longman, 1975), p5.
10. Ibid., p140.

VIII

MAN'S TRUE NATURE

MAN'S SPIRITUAL IDENTITY
AND HIS HUMAN ROLE ON EARTH

I said to the almond tree, 'Sister, speak to me of God.'
And the almond tree blossomed.
(Nikos Kazantzakis, *St. Francis*)

THE HUMAN PERSONA of man[1], through his body, his being and his very presence, inspires interrogatives: Who is man? What is the nature of his human nature? How did he come into existence? Why does he exist and where is he headed? Yet, beyond these perennial enigmas of origin, center, meaning, and final end lie the profounder and more disturbing factors that strike at the core of our conscious existence. Is the human being merely a physical being that is the accidental product of spontaneous and chance contingencies, a being who has evolved through a process that appears to be a straight line leading from nowhere and heading into oblivion? Is man the symbolic image of a primordial first man of the Edenic Paradise who, through a slow process of spiritual

---

1. The author guardedly uses the term 'man' as the most reasonable stylistic way of coming to terms with the concept of the *insan* in Islam and other religious traditions. This is in keeping with the use of such terminology in traditional languages as with the Arabic *insan* to signify the idea of collective humanity as a prototype person as such. In this instance, the construct 'man' is used as a qualitative concept indicating a non-gender-specific archetype and proto-human symbol for this age. No prejudicial or sexist reference is intended.

evolution and the experience as fallen and traditional man, comes to rest full circle as the perfected being within a paradisal garden that the religions traditions promise the faithful?

Modern psychology[2] represents the study of humankind from the purely human point of view rather than the metaphysical point of view. It seeks solutions to modern-day problems through the humanities in general and through the sciences such as anthropology and sociology. In particular, modern-day psychology and the other social sciences are intended to provide an insight into the very concept of man and his human 'nature', without the authority of Heaven so to speak, and without the knowledge through revelation that the Divinity provides. The rebellion of humanity against Heaven that began during the Renaissance in the Western world has reached its logical conclusion during these times in the attitude of modern-day individuals who have invested everything in the power of human reason alone to sift through the data measured by the human senses in order to provide the definitive norm of what is real and what is unreal.

It seems that modern psychology represents the study of man through the judgement and reasoning of humans themselves and projects a conceptualization of the human being that excludes that which is most essential to the human condition, namely, the unifying principle of God and all that principle implies. A sacred psychology of man, on the other hand, represents the study of man based solely on knowledge of God that descends to humanity in the form of revelation and is made up of divine truths that are enduring and universal rather than human theories that often fluctuate with

---

2. Jung is considered the 'father' of modern psychology and *the* major influence in its development. He is sometimes credited with drawing upon the themes of sacred psychology in the traditions, but he was perfectly capable of making statements, such as the following: 'Psychology...treats all metaphysical claims and assertions as mental phenomena, and regards them as statements about the mind and its structure that derive ultimately from certain unconscious dispositions. It does not consider them to be absolutely valid or even capable of establishing a metaphysical truth' (C.G. Jung, *The Collected Works of C.G. Jung*, p481). To call metaphysical truths 'unconscious dispositions' must represent a fundamental failure of 'spiritual' intelligence on his part, to say the least.

the ideological fashion of the times. Traditional people, who understood themselves to be basically spiritual beings, worshipped the Divine Being with a faith and a vigilance that implied an inward seeing with the *eye of the heart* (*'ayn al-qalb*), a direct and convincing vision if there ever was one. In the present time cycle, however, as we prepare ourselves psychologically to cross the threshold into the new century as well as the next millennium, we act *as if* we were purely psychological beings who define ourselves and find our meaning through human reasoning, memory, and imagination alone.[3] In the contemporary view, the psychological aspect of human life is reflective of a purely mental process which is in fact an extension of physical energies rendered profoundly mental somehow through machinations of neural phenomena interfacing with the human psyche.

According to the major religious traditions, human nature identifies man 'as such'. In principle, the Muslim, the Buddhist, or the Christian is not contemporary man or psychological man, primitive man or modern man.[4] The traditional man is man as such, a being that abides by the human nature he has been endowed with by the Supreme Intelligence. The faithful identify themselves according to an inward nature that is based upon the knowledge of God that has been delivered to humanity through multiple revelations. Because of the manner in which they identify themselves and who they understand themselves to be, human beings have the ability to transcend their earthly limitations and identify themselves as the Christian primordial man, the Taoist true man, the Buddhist universal man, and ultimately the perfected man (*al-insan al-kamil*) of the Islamic tradition. In other words, according to sacred psychology,

---

3. No one understood better than Jung, possibly the most respected of 20th century psychiatrists, the limitations of modern psychology and the dilemma of the modern-day psychologist. The object of psychology is the psychic; unfortunately it is also its subject (C. G. Jung, *Psychologie und Religion*, p61). This would be tantamount to saying that traditional man could understand the workings of his soul only by means of his own soul without the support of Heaven. For the psychologist, Jung confesses, the soul '...precisely belongs to the psychic and to nothing else' (ibid).

4. Nor is he evolutionary man, Marxist man, or Freudian man.

we are 'man as such',[5] capable in essence of rising above his earthly and contingent selfhood in order to know the true nature of reality. His nature reflects the human totality and is satisfied only with the Total. He is the mirror in which the names and attributes of God are reflected.

A truly sacred psychology of man originates in the primordial time, in what some traditions refer to as the 'Golden Age', in which humans was understood according to their true nature, with reference to their truly human nature. It is a psychology of man that sinks its roots into a revelation from the divine Source of all essential knowledge and seeks to unlock the secrets that human beings contain within the very ground of their souls. 'All is contained definitively in our own soul, whose lower ramifications are identified with the realm of the senses but whose root reaches up to pure being and the supreme essence, so that man grasps in himself the axis of the cosmos.'[6]

Needless to say, if the revelation refers primarily to the knowledge of God and secondarily to a knowledge of human 'nature', then a sacred psychology of man must refer initially to that divine knowledge and its corresponding human behavior in order to fulfil its role as a tool in the exploration of the human mind; not, however, a fragmented human behavior that is incapable of revealing deeper aspects of human nature. 'The study of fragmented behavior without a vision of the human nature which is the cause of this behavior cannot itself lead to knowledge of human nature. It can go around the rim of the wheel indefinitely without ever entering upon the spoke to approach the proximity of the axis and the Center. But if the vision is already present, the gaining of knowledge of external human behavior can always be an occasion for recollection

5. Man 'as such' departs from the Creator and Source as an individual and unique soul creation. 'Mankind! Fear and have reverence for your Lord, who created you from a single soul' (4:1).

6. J. Needleman (ed.), *The Sword of Gnosis*, p124. Although outwardly a small microcosm, man contains within him a reality that originates with the source of the cosmos itself. 'Soon We shall show them Our signs on the horizons of the earth and within their own souls, until it becomes clear to them that this is the Truth' (41:53).

and a return to the cause by means of the external effort.'[7] The revelation offers an essential knowledge of who God is and who man is, including their respective natures. In addition, this knowledge clarifies our position in relation to God and the other beings such as angels, devils and jinn within the universe, so that we can understand our place within the great hierarchy of being. Islam, and more specifically the *Sunnah* and *Hadith* literature featuring the sayings of the Prophet, offers a behavioral knowledge that amounts to being a sacred psychology of man. It allows human beings to be most truly themselves as they was intended to be, and provides a psychological basis through which they can transcend the limitations of both themselves and their own limited knowledge in order to achieve the perfection of soul and salvation of spirit in a paradisal reality that the human entity is destined in principle to achieve.

This is not to say that religion is *de facto* a sacred psychology, but it contains the elements of a psychology of man inasmuch as the religion reveals a concept of humanity that identifies their nature as primordial, permanent, universal and complete. In the Islamic perspective, man is his own priest and therefore in a sense his own psychologist, permitting a sacerdotal role for every person that brings the sacred psychology of man into the routine of daily life, thereby uniting the individual with the universal even on the most mundane level of daily existence, and thus sanctifying it. In addition to a metaphysical doctrine, the Quran also offers the Muslim a spiritual identity. The mind comes fully equipped with an intellect and a free will to respond to the principial knowledge of the revelation.

The form of the religion contains the structural framework and offers a methodology of action with which human beings can discipline themselves, come to know themselves, and ultimately transcend the limitations of their personal consciousness without compromising the expansion of a heightened spiritual awareness. Once again, a famous saying of the prophet—'He who knows himself will know his Lord'—already emphasizes the truth that we must look within toward our own human nature in order to understand

---

7. S.H. Nasr, *Islam and the Plight of Modern Man* (London: Longman, 1975), p5.

both ourselves and the Creator,[8] otherwise we would never advance along the line of a true spiritual evolution, nor could we achieve ultimate transcendence of our individual nature toward the universal truth, but rather would commence a spiral descent into the netherworld of psychological turmoil and spiritual darkness that is the genuine prelude to damnation of soul.

The question concerning the spiritual identity of man and his true inward nature—who is man?—is a question that modern psychology cannot rightly answer; whereas the spiritual perspective need not necessarily raise the question for the very reason that it so readily provides a coherent meaning and a corresponding spiritual identity that, while relating fully to the individual, is also universal and complete. It is true that our 'supra-natural' nature is not as immediately apparent as are objects in the physical world that can be verified by the efficiency of scientific observation;[9] but it is perfectly comprehensible, unlike the purely physical world which stares us in the face as it were but in reality offers no fully comprehensive explanation of itself.

Human nature is nothing short of a hidden disclosure consisting of four crucial elements that lend color and shades of meaning to the conceptualization of the human self-identity. These elements serve as open doors to the perception of human nature and thus

---

8. Similarly, the *Tao Te Ching* (xix) states: 'Realize thy Simple Self. Embrace thy Original Nature. Goal of man, knowledge of self, and who he is in reality.' And in another section of the *Tao* (xxxiii), we read: 'He who knows others is wise; He who knows himself is enlightened.' Socrates likewise daringly proclaimed: 'Know thyself.' And to quote a medieval Western contemplative: 'If the mind would fain ascent to the height of Science, let it's first and principal study be to know itself' (Richard of St. Victor).

9. According to F. Schuon, the 'sacred sciences' such as revelation and symbolism need not adjust themselves to the modern scientific approach in the verification of objective knowledge. 'The realm of revelation, of symbolism, of pure and direct intellection, stands in fact above both the physical and psychological realms, and consequently it lies beyond the scope of so called scientific methods. If we feel we cannot accept the language of traditional symbolism, because to us it seems fanciful and arbitrary, this shows we have not yet understood that language, and certainly not that we have advanced beyond it' F. Schuon, 'No Activity without Truth', *Studies in Comparative Religion*, Autumn 1969, vol. 3, no. 4.

lead to an understanding of the nature of reality itself. Based on the Quranic revelation, but also conforming to the other monotheistic spiritual traditions, human nature or *fitrah* is traditionally characterized as primordial, permanent, theomorphic, and universal.

The word *fitrah* in its Arabic root can be understood to refer to the human 'norm' from which, according to the Quran, humanity has fallen away. Having been fashioned from the creative 'hand' of God, primordial man was innocent, pure, true, free, virtuous, and understood his true place in the great hierarchy of being. The Quran is quite specific in its references to man's inner nature when an important verse says: 'So set thy face steadily and truly to religion, Allah's handiwork according to the nature on which He has created mankind. No change (let there be) in the work (wrought) by Allah: That is the standard religion, but most men know it not' (30:30). It reveals that the nature of humanity has been patterned on the nature of God (*fitrah Allah*) in terms of its original inception, and this of course cannot be altered in any respect.

Natural man, then, is already perfect man in principle, even if perfection does not come naturally to man because of the consequence of the fall from the paradisal garden. Before his fall from grace, Adam was considered primordial because he already enjoyed the perfection inherent within human nature and he saw and understood the world from within. In other words, primordial man was the embodiment of a living spirituality.[10] The modern person can still claim a primordial nature in so far as he/she continues to enjoy the same inner nature that Adam and Eve exemplified in principle, once this nature is coupled with the aspiration to return to the original purity that people today are still capable of because of who they are in principle.

Primordiality already adds a spiritual dimension to the human being that modern psychology does not even admit to as a matter of basic premise. The modern psyche is understood to have an 'infra-

---

10. Schuon emphasizes the importance of the primordial man within the modern man: 'to realize the "Ancient" or "Primordial" man means to return to the origin which we bear within us; it means to return to eternal childhood, to rest in our archetype, in our primordial and normative form, or in our theomorphic substance,' *Understanding Islam*, tr. D.M. Matheson (NY: Penguin Books, 1972), p102.

natural' origin, arising as it does from below, while the traditional psyche was always understood to be 'supra-natural' in nature, descending as it did from above. Needless to say, it should be noted that neither the Quran nor the sayings of the Prophet (*hadith*) offer us a flattering picture of human nature as it exists on earth, nor does the existential experience of living in today's world help us to understand man as primordial, pristine, and pure. The psychological challenge in today's world, as it has always been down through the ages, is to conform to what we are according to our true nature, however much this may elude our grasp within the existential, earthly reality.

Be that as it may, beyond humanity's primordiality, which retains and still represents an ambiance of infancy and first origins, lies the permanence of their true nature, a nature which is unchanging in its basic construct since the beginning of the primordial era witnessed during the Golden Age. Human nature partakes of permanence which began in the primordial era of the Edenic Garden and which the soul takes with it on its journey of return to God. This idea also sharply contradicts the prevailing evolutionary concept that man has somehow evolved, not only as a physical form but presumably also in the psychological and psychic capacity within human nature itself, from a lower to a higher species. However, this runs counter to the spiritual perspective that admits only of a descent from higher to lower levels and rejects any suggestion of an ascent from lower to higher levels of existence.

In this view, humans understand themselves to be 'extra-spatial' and 'extra-temporal' in nature in which they contain elements that are constant and permanent, and this is none other than an aspect of the *fitrah Allah* or true nature because God's nature is true. As such, the human norm is characterized by permanence. Thus, the goal of all human spirituality is to recognize and to return to that norm, to the permanent and original nature or *fitrah*, according to the Islamic perspective. The question of who man is and how he identifies himself begins with the consideration of the characteristics that the revelation identifies man's human nature to be.

In addition, human nature is considered to be theomorphic in the spiritual perspective because it originates in God and is distinguished by the qualities that God has imbued humans with. Man can be a mirror of the divine attributes and qualities because of his theomorphic nature, which asks us to be and to behave in accordance with who we truly are. A theomorphic nature requires humans to be true to themselves according to their true nature and not to forget their 'original' nature. An important aspect of a theomorphic nature is the fact that humans have been given knowledge that the angels don't partake of. The Quran teaches us that Adam learned 'the names of things' (2:31) which means that he understood implicitly the inner nature and quality of things in their essence. Even though we try to float on the surface of our being, far from our own center, being made in the image of God reminds us that we are the theophany of God's names and qualities. This is a reality that lies at the center of the human condition.

Finally, to say that human nature is universal means to imply that it is based on a prototype of humanity that transcends time and space and provides the balance to the eternal aspect of human nature. Universal man is both the true man of Taoism and the perfect man of Islam, true in so far as he reflects the qualities and attributes of the primordial man and perfect in so far as he reflects the nature of the prophet in reflection to the nature of the Divine Being. Muslims imitate the Prophet both outwardly and inwardly, so that they can model and identify their own individual nature with the human nature of the Prophet. Thus, they have the potential of knowing themselves and enjoy a full conceptualization of humanity by imitating the prototype of human nature as exemplified in the Prophet, who in the Islamic context is the perfect man (al-insan al-kamil). It is said that to enter into the mold of the prophet's personality through the Sunnah and the Hadith is to enter into the very mold of the Quran, since his nature was the nature of the Quran.[11] In this way, human nature can approximate the nature of God, through the revelation implicit within the mind and heart,

11. It is part of the immense impact of the Quran that considering our 'fallen nature', it 'restores to us the condition of fitrah. It gives back to the intelligence its lost capacity to perceive and to comprehend supernatural truths, it gives back to the will its lost capacity to command the warring factions in the soul, and it gives back to sentiment its lost capacity to love God and to love everything that reminds us of Him.' Eaton, Islam and the Destiny of Man, p78.

through the words and the example of the Prophet, and through the revealed knowledge of the Quran.

(((

IT IS PRECISELY BECAUSE humanity has such an inborn and fixed nature that they can effectively fulfil the dual roles of both representative (*khalifah*) and slave (*abd*) of God on earth. Along with the possibility of a pure and innocent nature lies the responsibility as an earthly being with an attitude of servitude toward his Creator. "'Behold,' the Lord said to the angels: "I will create a vicegerent on the earth." And the angels said: "Will You place therein one who will create trouble and shed blood, while we celebrate Your praises and glorify Your holy Name." And God replied: "I know what you do not know."' (2:30)

Since all Muslims are considered to be their own priest and therefore the celebrant of the sacred rituals of formal worship, their sacerdotal character is no more meaningfully demonstrated than in their role as God's earthly representative. Precisely by exercising their duty as God's viceroy on earth, Muslims come to realize the importance of their role as the servant of God, a role that is implicit in their existential experience on earth. In order that humans can fully understand themselves as *the* thinking being in God's creation, they must contain within themselves two awesome possibilities: Supreme significance as the *khalifah* of God on earth, and utter insignificance in the role of *abd* whose abject servitude is fundamental to their inability to be otherwise in the hierarchy of the cosmic universe. In the microcosmic human world, the human beings are both master and representative of themselves and their environment, while at the same time they are the humble servants of their Lord. These two modes of expression complement one another and enhance the human experience, however paradoxical and contradictory that may seem. The earthly representative of God cannot function properly without a clear understanding that he/she is also the human servant of God; the polarity is such that in order to comprehend one's strengths, one's limitations must also be recognized.

It is a *de facto* condition of being a human rather than a divine being.

As *khalifah*, humans are able to rediscover themselves as having been created *in the best of forms* (95:4). The heart can become like a well-polished mirror[12] in which the divine names and qualities can be reflected. It is indeed the spiritual ideal of the religion of Islam to transform the human soul of the Muslim into a pure crystal reflecting the Divine Light. As *abd* (slave), the human *insan* is also understood in Islam to be a creature of dust and clay and a slave, 'a nothingness before the overwhelming splendor of the Real— impotent before Omnipotence, a little thing (brother to the ant) who walks briefly upon the earth from which he was molded, vulnerable to a pinprick and destined soon to be seized upon and taken to Judgment.'[13]

This conceptualization of humanity reflects a psychology that is well-nigh spiritual in so far as the projection of the Divine Being into the human being is conceived on all levels, just as the spiritual world is superimposed on the human world, just as the vertical dimension continuously intersects the horizontal plane, adding a fourth dimension of spirituality to a three dimensional world manifested as the science of forms.

Master and slave are two earthly modalities that lend a profound coloration to understanding not only the place of humans in the hierarchy of being, higher than the angels yet capable of damnation because of who they are and what they are capable of. The master needs the slave in order to complete his own role as master, just as vicegerency itself is inevitably linked to slavery. They are two faces of the same coin, two attitudes that lend perspective and meaning to the human condition. According to the mystic al-Ghazzali (d. 505 / AD 1111), everything including the

12. In your seeing your true self, He is your mirror and you are His mirror in which He sees His Names and their determination, which are nothing other than Himself' Ibn al-Arabi, The *Bezels of Wisdom* trans. R.W.J. Austin, (New York: Paulist Press, 1980) p65). On the traditional meaning of the symbolism of the mirror, see T. Burckhardt, *The Mirror of the Intellect*, chap. 10, 1987.

13. *Islamic Spirituality: Foundations*, Seyyed Hossein Nasr (ed.), chap. 19, 'Man', Charles le Gai Eaton (New York: Crossroad, 1987), p359.

human creature has 'a face of its own and a face of its Lord; in respect of its own face it is nothingness, and in respect of the face of its Lord it is Being.' Within the Islamic context, if people do not understand that the human identity contains these two elements, then they have failed to understand the reality of their existential situation in which they have the intelligence and free will to act as God's representative, without forgetting the corresponding humility that acknowledges man's place with respect to the Absolute.

In view of these two modalities, humanity is understood to be both a mirror and a bridge. Humans are a bridge to the Divine Being in their role as God's agent and spokesman. Through intelligence and free will, they, of all the created beings, are capable of conceiving of God, comprehending the divine significance, and acting upon that knowledge to achieve a realization through an experience well lived and ultimately internalized. They are called *Homo sapiens*, Allah's thinking creature and the masterpiece of His creation. They are fashioned by God's own hand and He has breathed into him of His Spirit.[14] They are conscious of themselves, and as much as that consciousness refers back to the Divine Being, then they are also objective and absolute in a subjective and relative world. Man is *insan*,[15] the one who accepted the sacred trust; he was taught and knows the names of things; the angels bowed down before him, and through prayer he can speak his aspirations and hopes and communicate internally with God.

When Muslims see their reflection in the Divine Mirror, they see God's slave. Indeed, their intelligence demands that they recognize their nothingness in the face of the Divine Reality as an earthly reality and not just as a vague sentimentality, and their free will proves this again and again by conforming to the Divine Will through surrender and virtue. They are creatures of dust, subjective beings, in transient and in exile from the paradise that Adam deliberately

---

14. Behold I am about to create a man from sounding clay and mounted into a shape, and I have fashioned him in due proportion and breathed into him of My Spirit' (15:28).

15. It is said that the Arabic word for man, *insan*, is derived from the root *uns*, which means 'intimacy' Nasr [ed.], *Islamic Spirituality: Foundations*, p363.

turned his back on through pride and forgetfulness. Is this not reason enough for abject humility before the Divine Magnitude? When Muslims see their reflection in the earthly mirror, they see God's representative on earth. Indeed, their intelligence, free will, and virtue all point to a responsible being who must ultimately give an account of their actions and intentions and who fully accept this responsibility. Once again, he is *insan*, a being capable of rising above his earthly and contingent self and capable of knowing the reality. His nature reflects totality and he is ultimately satisfied only with the totality that is represented in God.

The proper balance of these two roles of vicegerency and slavery makes it possible for the human being to be described as a central being who already enjoys a human nature that is both perfect and pure in principle. Because Muslims are both a mirror and a bridge, they have the power to transcend all earthly limitations through the overwhelming possibilities of the Divine Reality. As *khalifah*, they are a world (microcosm) within a world (macrocosm); as *abd*, they are but an instrument in the Hand of God. Through the modalities of *khalifah* and *abd*, they become confluently a contradiction and a paradox, a well-balanced complementarity of both master and slave, a meeting place and a bridge.

(((

A WORD IN THIS CONTEXT needs to be said about prayer, because human nature and spiritual identity come together as a unified force of personal intimacy between the human and the Divine through prayer, thereby justifying the *uns* (intimacy) of the Islamic *insan* (man). The entire creation, including the plant and animal kingdoms, praises God out of an instinctive knowledge; but only the human being can consciously praise the Divine Being through active worship and humble service. The role of prayer in the human context is an exhaustive subject that we will mention here only in passing[16] since it strikes such a deep cord with human nature and

16. We have written on this subject more extensively in another context. See our earlier work *Veils and Keys: Possibilities for a Contemporary Spirituality in the*

plays such a significant role in our spiritual identity. The ritual of prayer, together with the other spiritual practices still available to people the world over, permits an expression of self as the natural outpouring of all their inner thoughts, hopes and aspirations with regard to the Supreme Being who created them.

In Islam, the ritual form of the prayer and the latent power of the sacred Quranic language uttered in the prayer ritual are able to achieve a goal which the psychoanalyst seeks to accomplish with dubious success and instead often produces only dangerous results, for he/she lacks the power of the Spirit of God which alone can guide the human soul. Through prayer, the aspirants expose themselves to the mercy (*rahmah*) and the blessing (*barakat*) of God. By virtue of the role as *khalifah*, the Muslim is permitted to come into the presence of the Divine Being. Once there in that sublime Presence, however, the human being must become the image of humility, the ultimate slave in awe of the Master, hands folded and head bowed.

I am with (My servant) when he remembers Me. If he makes mention of Me to himself, I make mention of him to Myself. . . . . And if he draws near to Me a hand's span, I draw near to him an arm's length; and if he draws near to me an arm's length, I draw near to him a fathom's length. And if he comes to Me walking, I go to him speedily (*hadith qudsi*).

Seen in this light, a sacred psychology within the context of a spiritual tradition such as Islam is nothing short of a sacred science designed as a cure for the ailments of the soul. It has the capacity to untie the knots that entangle the human mind and prevent it from coming into close proximity with the Spirit. In traditional literature, this process was often referred to as spiritual alchemy, representing a transformation of the psyche from the base metal that it is in reality to the golden light that it is in principle. This is actually what we call today psychotherapy, and is far superior to any modern

Light of Traditional Islamic Wisdom (Kuala Lumpur, Malaysia: Noordeen Publications, 1998), chap. 7, 'The Significance of Prayer and its Implications for Humanity'.

psychotherapy, which claims to cure the psychic and spiritual ills of man without the healing power of the Spirit of God.

The doctrine of the implicit reality of a Divine Being set out in the spiritual traditions sheds light on the doctrine of humanity to the extent that they are clearly identified in the revelation as human beings in view of the Divine Being. Humans are nothing before the Divine Majesty, but they are also the representatives of God on earth by virtue of their theomorphic nature that can reflect the names and qualities of God within this world. In Islam, Muslims are the intimates of God and a living symbol of all that can be 'divinely human' in the world. Because of their primordial nature, they have the capacity of becoming perfect once again as in the image of the universal man. Although in reality we are still far from that ideal, this does not deny us the possibility of attempting to become what we are intended to be and are in essence. This is at the heart of a sacred psychology of man, a true psychology that identifies who man is, places him within the center of the self and provides a means through spiritual discipline and the corresponding channels of blessing that will reconstitute the human soul with a primordial purity that is the prerequisite of the paradisal state.

At one time, everything was a sign and a symbol, indeed a proof of the existence of God and served as meaningful signposts to the spiritual realities. The seven heavens themselves offered a vast panorama of cosmic possibility and were inhabited by an entire hierarchy of beings including angels and jinn, but that alas has now been reduced to a series of astronomical theories and facts that prevent man from recognizing the divine signs therein. 'For nothing now reminds him that after all this whole universe is contained in him, not indeed in his individual being, but in the spirit that is in him and that is at the same time more than himself and more than the entire phenomenal universe.'[17]

When we gaze upon the dark plate of the night sky, we view the kernel of a truth that lies simultaneously within our very being. We must discover our own meaning once again, and this is made

17. Titus Burckhardt, 'Cosmology and Modern Science', in *The Sword of Gnosis*, ed. J. Needleman (Baltimore, MD: Penguin, 1974), p138.

possible through a sacred psychology already embodied within the principles of knowledge and methods of devotion of the religions. These principles permit human beings to escape their existential and psychological limitations through a faith in the Reality of the Divine Being, a faith that leads to the surrender of the human will to the Divine Will, a faith that can replace the limitations of a self-serving and externalized ego with the inner sanctuary of the soul and spirit which alone can contain the mystery implicit in the universe.

The Divine Affirmation that is implicit in the testimony of faith in the one God is the liberating 'yes' to a reality that exists within us as microcosm, reflects within the macrocosm, and then extends far beyond any known horizon toward the metacosmos. To make this sacred affirmation, to know God and to want to love Him, brings to the surface an impulse that lies embedded within man's nature, namely to proclaim the truth that humanity is most truly human just as God is most truly Divine. Implicit in the religions and their sacred traditions is a sacred psychology that has the power to shatter lower impulses, untie psychological knots, and bring together the multiple fragments of man into a unity that already lies in the ground of his soul as a primordial legacy and as a revelatory promise.

IX

BEHIND THE FACE OF MAN

INSIDE THE WELL OF HUMAN CONSCIOUSNESS

All men know how to seek for what they do not know,
But nobody seems to know how to seek for what is already known.
(The Book of Chuang Tzu)

BEYOND THE CONSIDERATION of human nature and beyond the concept of humanity as the human representative of God on earth (*khalifah*) and the humble slave (*abd*) of the Divinity lies the mystery of human consciousness: What it is precisely, how it originated, what purpose it serves, and to what end it will lead humanity. Beyond the face of modern man and beyond the grasp of the modern scientific inquiry lies the enigmatic knowledge of the self, a universal mystery whose integrity as a perennial enigma has succeeded in preserving the defining quality of humanity's humanness from the knife-edge of irreverent scientific scrutiny. Human consciousness continues to define the humanity within us in ways that still elude the comprehension of the modern scientific community.

We know from the religious traditions that human consciousness represents a state of mind and a higher cognitive faculty that raises the human being above the rest of the creation to become the human reflection of the ninety-nine names of the Divine Being, this being one of the meanings of the term 'made in the image of God'. What we perhaps don't remember, by virtue of the offensive of modern science to reduce the human mind to a mechanized analogue emerging out of the neurons of inorganic brain matter, is that in mirroring the Supreme Mind, human consciousness becomes a supra-sensory faculty that permits these divine qualities and attributes to become existential realities and virtues that characterize the humanness of man in the light of these higher spiritual attributes. We need to reflect upon and consider what the traditional mentality has known all along and what the modern mentality is not willing to admit, namely that consciousness is an artifact of the mind that irradiates the entire thinking process and links us directly to the Spirit that encompasses the cosmos.

We noted in an earlier chapter that the design of the entire creation—and the purpose of the creation of man by way of implication—came into being and began to exist because the Mind of God, the Divine Consciousness if you will, desired to be known by His thinking creation, recalling the familiar *hadith qudsi* in which Allah speaks directly through the Prophet: 'I was a hidden treasure and wanted to become known. Therefore, I created the universe.' The creation of Adam, therefore, implies above all the creation of a human consciousness that identifies the human being as human and that serves as a supra-natural zone of awareness that makes direct communication between the mind of man and the Mind of God at all possible. As the essential element to the functioning of our humanity, we have an abstract and complete superstructure available containing layers of mind and degrees of awareness that are as subtle and all-encompassing as the cosmic spheres mounted within the universe. Indeed, consciousness represents a subtle field of experience whose degrees and layers need to be peeled back in order to reveal the 'vertical dimension' that leads toward inner, spiritual growth, as the individual touches within himself the fundamental force-field whose reflective intelligence resonates with the energy and spirit of the Divine Consciousness.

Because of the many levels and degrees that are usually associated with the faculty of human consciousness, it could be called the spectrum of the mind whose many colors and shades actually provide the prism through which we consider the machinations of the inner self and understand the reality of the world we live in. Nothing highlights more the interaction of the human world as microcosm and the world of the universe as macrocosm as does the mystery of consciousness. The Supreme Consciousness of the Divine Being expressed the desire 'to be known', thereby creating the living reality of the universe and the presence and state of mind of the human consciousness as a complement to that desire. Against this cosmic background of self-awareness, the conscious—as opposed to the animal—mind serves as a kind of witness that transcends both humanity and the world by being a quality of thought that allows experience to be viewed through a transcending mirror that witnesses the essential knowledge of God through a reflection of the self. Without this self-reflective faculty, animals theoretically have no past and no future, at least not in the way that we do. They live instinctively within the present moment and the intelligence given their station serves them well to meet the contingencies of their environment, even if they cannot 'see' themselves or understand their origin and destiny. In other words, they are not subjects who are capable of objectivity and they cannot capture the essence of things. Because of human consciousness, only the *Homo sapiens* participates in the transcendent principle and reflects a luminous source, otherwise our species would be like the animals, living for the moment but with no past and no future.

That having been said, however, it must be added that consciousness lurks as an unexplained mystery in the shadow of the human form. Even though we rely on its multi-faceted power and innate ability, we speak with reservation about the meaning of consciousness, and yet our reservation is fraught with the wisdom that lies in the shadow of a seemingly conscious universe. It recalls the color of the rainbow with its transparent hint of miracle reaching down and touching earth before disappearing again in the mist. It reflects wisdom behind the flight of the eagle. It remembers the perfection within the design of snow crystals and the calm within the eye of the storm. It summons the beauty encompassed within the colorful forms of a butterfly wing, and the message of order and design behind the spider's web. Indeed, consciousness synthesizes a web of intricacies that encaptures all of nature and places man at the heart of it all as the one observing and listening, in search of a knowledge that lies within the cells of our being as it does beyond the outer reaches of the stars.

The depth of human consciousness, according to the early traditions of Buddhism as well as modern depth psychology, reaches back to a beginningless past with the entire universe as its basis, when consciousness became manifest as a conscious awakening to knowledge and to life. Consciousness became known to Adam when he first met himself in the dawn of his life. As a purely subjective being, he did not say: 'I am I'; but rather, as a subjective being capable of objectivity, he was able to say 'I am not I but He that is in me'[1], as if he could gaze within the well of his own being and see not himself but the Divinity that created him. In this way, his intelligence became reflective and objectifying, as the individual consciousness of his ego re-oriented itself away from the purely physical and corporeal world toward its luminous source in the lofty realm of the Spirit. For humanity, consciousness began long ago in a far away place in the blue-white morning of the human mind. Consequently, the primordial resonance of dawn shines down through the ages of time as a crystalline quality of comprehensibility that characterizes the state of mind associated with consciousness, a brilliant clarity and a heightened presence that provides the protocol and ambiance for all human thought.

Thereafter, humanity has lived as a human being through the power of a unique consciousness. We are human man rather than hominoid man because of the defining quality of our consciousness. We have within us the potential to transcend ourselves through a heightened consciousness that will lead us back to the white light of eternity that is traditionally referred to as enlightenment. As the generations of humanity have proceeded down through the millennia, the ways and paths of the religions have whispered to us of the single requirement that makes us what we are as human beings on earth and as universal beings by nature and in principle, namely the ability to see ourselves as individual identities and to know ourselves as a mirror reflection of a Superior Being. We are beings who live 'self-consciously' in time but who exist 'supraconsciously' within the eternal moment. As *Homo sapiens*, human

---

1. A kind of human *shahadah* or testimony, in remembrance of the Islamic *shahadah* that denies the world in order to affirm the Supreme Being in Allah.

intelligence is related to consciousness as time is related to eternity. As *Homo spiritualis*, to live in time is to live within the context of eternity; while to be intelligent is to take part in a consciousness that transcends the human order. There exists something in humanity whose reality belongs to an order beyond time; there exists within humanity the consciousness of a reality that can envisage not only time, but also its origin in eternity and its final end, not in a terminal moment but in transcendence.

The five senses define the elements of 'this world' but remember and reflect the qualities of the 'other world'. Our eyes see clearly and we look directly at the reality of the world, but we remember the reality of a higher world. We hear and comprehend the voice of language and the sound of nature, but remember the voice of God. We smell the odors of life, but remember the presence of otherworldly spirits through perfume and incense. Through speech, we can articulate the narrative of our mind, and through the sense of touch we can communicate with others in this world and express the higher emotions of the spirit-world.

The ways of the spirit whisper to us at the dawn of day, in the final moments before sleep, in times of crisis, during moments of prayer. The ways of the spirit make themselves known when all the existential barriers have suddenly fallen away and the veils separating us from a direct perception of the true reality have been lifted. The way of the spirit reveals a conscious awakening of the human self-awakening that feels like something has cracked open inside and poured its revelatory contents over the surface of the mind. What it is or means exactly we do not know, but it recreates the qualities of mind that we experience as fully human beings but cannot adequately explain. The mindfulness of thought, the supreme logic of reason, the force of human will, the prescient awareness, the abiding vision of the self, and the ability to conceptualize objectively and objectify our subjective experience are all the result of this outpouring of higher consciousness. Ultimately, the faint echoes of the supreme consciousness emerge and make their presence felt, recalling primordial man and anticipating the perfect and universal man referred to in Islam.

We experience directly a structure associated with consciousness, a structure whose design is well ordered and subtle and whose power is unique and infinite. We have a knowledge within us that is encased in consciousness; it is not a thing to be studied or explained, but rather a process to be experienced. There is a mystery to consciousness on the one hand that leaves us questioning its ultimate meaning, and there is clarity on the other hand that answers all questions and resolves all doubt. It calls upon the bottomless depths of an ancient well that at the same time has the power to lead us beyond the border of our known selves. Drop a stone into this well and you listen to its descent into depths that know no arrival. It reaches its pinnacle of manifestation when we sense a thing without knowing it and know a thing without consciously perceiving it. The knowledge has become realized within our being and its presence is known and felt as an existential as well as an inner reality. It is an awareness that seizes the body and reaches down to the level of the cells even, and it is a mindfulness that seeps into the mind and psyche as an ethereal mist, revealing a presence that identifies who we are and a power that leads ultimately to transcendence of self.

The conscious mind that once drew primitive images of people and animals on a cave wall in the south of France has been an active witness to its own historical development in a vast narrative of progression and change that has taken modern scientists to places they will never visit in person. Through instruments of their own devising, their mechanical eye gazes many millions of light years into the far reaches of the heavens and their radio ears listen to the whisperings of even more remote galaxies. With the aid of sophisticated microscopes, they are able to dissect the elements of their own being and through great particle accelerators, they can (indirectly) observe the actions and consequences of the particles of sub-atomic matter. Because of a formidable, inquiring mind and the unique character of his consciousness, modern scientists have broken through the boundaries that control and limit the rest of the creation and allowed them to reach a level of speculation and thought never before envisioned in the history of humankind.

Consciousness represents a continuum that cannot be denied. Memory fades; imagination falters; reason deceives; logic fails. Our intelligence can fall short of the mark and our desires and emotions change with the wind. Still, consciousness is always there—like the air to the wind, the glow to the fire, the darkness to the night, the peak to the wave and the bud to the flower. It is there because it is the necessary foundation upon which we are built, a mystery that is dark and rich and enduring, and that shares in the wisdom of the universe.

Without consciousness, we would not be human; with it we can know the Divinity and reflect His names and qualities.

(((

UNDERSTANDING HUMAN CONSCIOUSNESS is a fundamental problem in today's world. In spite of the huge advances we have achieved in both scientific and technical knowledge, most notably through the capacity and power of the mind, human consciousness still remains the enigmatic phantom that haunts the periphery of the human mind and psyche with its unexplained presence, raising serious considerations that strike at the heart of our perception of self. To raise the question of consciousness is to invite people living in today's world to consider an aspect of themselves for which they no longer have any clear guidelines, bereft as they are now of the vision of the human being as a conscious and enlightened being portrayed within the scriptures of the world religions as being made in the image of God and reflecting the higher consciousness of the Mind of God. Within the traditional perspective of the world religions, the idea of a human consciousness that reflected somehow the consciousness of a Supreme Being virtually defined the parameters within which traditional man was able to function as a human being.

At the heart of the deliberations concerning the human mind and the consciousness that shapes and illuminates that mind is the fact that modern scientists are confronted with the dilemma of putting the abstract and intangible notion of human consciousness—a consciousness most notably that makes human thought possible as an active and self-aware process rather than merely the instinctive drive found in animal intelligence—within the framework of the scientific worldview with its reliance on the objective principle of matter and the ability of the rational and presumably conscious mind to verify given realities within a framework of principles and laws of nature based on the mind itself and the matter that substantiates the created universe. Needless to say, the mind and the subtle ambiance of its consciousness escape the scrutiny of modern science even to the extent that scientists are unable to establish a simple definition with any consensus. The truth is that modern science does not know what consciousness is within the framework that it abides by, even though modern scientists know that it exists by virtue of their own experience of self-awareness, presence of mind, and the awesome powers of contemplation and creativity they experience and rely on, including flashes of intuition and insight that fuel the initial process of scientific inquiry.

When it comes to defining human consciousness, we moderns are left groping for words in spite of the fact that we feel it in our very bones as being the best of ourselves. Our minds would be nothing without it, nor could we identify or know ourselves in any feasible or comprehensive manner. As much as we like to speculate during this day and age concerning our link with the simian world and our potentially genetic lineage with chimps and the great apes, we have only to think of the limitations of the animal mind in order to realize what consciousness is by virtue of the huge and unbreachable barrier that exists between the human and the animal world. Behind the face of the ape lies the animal nature of the ape with its dark message of limitation and brutishness shining down through the ages of time. The primate world looks upon man from the edge of the forest, unable to pass through the door of perception into any kind of objective knowing or self-awareness. Chimps and apes are forever consigned to roam the corridors of their instinctive natures without departing from the borders of their true self.

Scientists seem to favor two fundamental approaches to the study of human consciousness: Studying the secrets revealed by fossil analysis and analyzing the physical activity of the brain.

Firstly, they search the fossil archives in order to trace a gradual evolutionary process in the development of the human mind through presumably many different species before ultimately arriving at the mental machinations of the primate world. They tend to view the evolution of consciousness as the third of the three great steps in the evolution of human growth, commencing with the development of bi-pedalism, followed by the origin of a sufficiently big brain to accommodate man's expansive mind, and finally the emergence of introspective consciousness as the pinnacle and synthesis in the development of the human mind. This has become possible, according to scientific speculation, through the process of a sudden 'cognitive efflorescence' of higher mind. The vastness of geologic time provides the framework within which virtually anything and everything becomes possible by virtue of a time factor that permits the gradual evolution of anything to develop. Thus, we learn from paleontologists, for example, that each member of the *Homo* family antecedent to *Homo sapiens* had a 'frisson of humanness' about it, not just in the growth of its stature and deportment, but in the way the developing mind actually worked. We are told, seriously and in earnest, that the 'beacon of humanness' burned increasingly more brightly somehow through the course of time, although what generated this 'beacon' and what process enhanced its development remains unidentified, until the light of the human mind illuminated the world with the 'glaring intensity' we now experience.

Secondly, scientists have resorted to searching the broad base and considerable activity of gray brain matter to find within the chill void of molecules and particles of the physical world the spark that allegedly initiated this cognitive efflorescence and fuels the inner glow of human consciousness.

In another corner of the scientific universe, neuroscientists have been trying to close the gap between brain and mind, to show that consciousness is simply an emergent property arising from brain cells, whose behavior can be explained with chemistry, the grammar of molecules and atoms. The mind arises from the laws of matter.[2]

2. George Johnson, *Fire in the Mind* (New York: Random House, 1995), p149. This is reductionism taken to its logical conclusion, in which the mystery of man's consciousness is reduced to nothing more than physical matter.

Obviously, feelings of ambivalence abound, as does a tenacity of spirit that paradoxically refuses to give up its reliance on the alleged objectivity of pure matter.

The renowned paleontologist Richard Leakey notes that although many functions can be identified within the brain, 'one of the remarkable features of this organ is that some functions, often important ones, defy precise locating. One of these is conscious-ness. No one has been able to point to a region of the brain and say, this exclusively is the seat of consciousness.'[3] However, like many other scientist who have placed their faith in evolution as the explanatory force in man's origin and development, including both a human culture and a consciousness that have 'emerged gradually through our history,' he ultimately admits that he takes the materi-alist view that 'consciousness is the product of the brain's activity, not some gossamer attachment to the organ, as the noted neurolo-gist Sir John Eccles recently suggested. 'I am constrained to attribute the uniqueness of the Self or Soul to a supernatural spiritual cre-ation,' he wrote in his latest book, *Evolution of the Brain.*' In the next sentence, he quickly adds that he is sympathetic to the sentiments expressed in a recent essay by Colin McGinn, a philosopher at Rut-gers University. 'How is it possible for conscious states to depend on brain states?' ponders McGinn. 'How can Technicolor phenomenol-ogy arise from soggy gray matter? What makes the bodily organ we call the brain so radically different from other bodily organs, say the kidneys—the body parts without a trace of consciousness? How could the aggregation of millions of individually insentient neurons generate subjective awareness? . . . Somehow, we feel, the water of the physical brain is turned into the wine of consciousness, but we draw a total blank on the nature of this conversion.'[4]

The focus of scientific inquiry now lies in the direction of how

3. Richard Leakey and Roger Lewin, *Origins Reconsidered: In Search of What Makes Us Human* (New York: Doubleday, 1992), p253.

4. Ibid., p281. No such ambivalence distinguishes the remarks of the evolution-ary reductionist Ernst Haeckel who wrote over a hundred years ago in 1877 that 'the cell consists of matter , , , composed chiefly of carbon with an admixture of hydro-gen, nitrogen and sulphur. These component parts, properly united produce the soul and body of the animated world, and suitably nourished become man. With

the brain generates the mind, since once the origin and mechanics of the mind have been identified, many scientists reckon, man's consciousness cannot be far behind. Francis Crick, co-discoverer of the molecular structure of dna in 1953, has suggested: 'You, your joys and your sorrows, your memories and your ambitions, your sense of personal identity and free will, are in fact no more than the behavior of a vast assembly of nerve cells and their associated mole-cules.'[5] It seems paradoxical to say the least that a mind of such technical brilliance can also express such a willingness to reduce the creative, emotive and altruistic heights of humanity to the purely arbitrary physical activity of molecules and cells without so much as an expression of regret for the lost consciousness of the universe. Nevertheless, this is the approach that modern science continues to take in its pursuit of an understanding of human consciousness. A consciousness that was once associated with light is now associated with brain images reflected in the workings of magnetic resonance imaging (mri) and positron emotion tomography (pet) which dis-play images of the brain at work. Well armed with the technical bril-liance of recent discoveries in molecular biology *et al*, in which the secrets underlying the biology of memory, perception and problem-solving are revealed, the question has now seriously been raised: 'Can the very mechanisms of consciousness itself be far behind?'[6]

It may surprise many scientists to learn that the answer to this question may ultimately be 'Yes!', not only left far, far behind but well beyond the horizon of knowability. We do not need to discover that we know; but how we know what we know is one of the great mysteries, indeed it is acknowledged to be *the* mystery of our time, perceived as an impenetrable enigma because everyone experiences consciousness, but no one can adequately define its properties and

---

this single argument the mystery of the universe is explained, the Deity annulled and a new era of infinite knowledge ushered in.' Quoted in Loren Eiseley's *The Star Thrower* (New York: Harcourt, Brace & Company, 1979), p191.

5. Perhaps he should write 'I' and 'my' rather than 'you' and 'your', thus liberat-ing the mass of humanity from this alarming inference. As quoted in a time special issue: The *New Age of Discovery*, 'A Clear Consciousness', Antonio R. Damasio, Winter 1997/98, pp88–90.

6. Ibid.

ultimate meaning. Still, one wonders what propels the modern mentality to try to reduce the mystery and the miracle embodied within the human mind to its lowest common denominator in the physical plane of the brain. Would it be reasonable or acceptable to reduce the mystery of the human smile to the geometry of lips, mouth and teeth? Can all the profound sorrow of humanity be summarized and 'explained away' by the chemicals of a human tear? What is it about our age and its narrow and closed mentality that chooses to believe in the reality of a 'thing', and not the soul or spirit that gives it life and meaning?

What is consciousness? We have the right to ask the modern world, a world that endeavors to cling to a long-outdated mechanistic worldview with no sense of self. Is it a biological artifact, an accident of evolution, or something deeply woven into the warp and woof of the universe? Obviously, this is a question, like the question of origins, that modern science feels very uncomfortable with. As the distinctive trait of the human being, a trait that virtually characterizes his humanness, does consciousness rest on the cognitive foundation of our apelike ancestors? Did it evolve gradually with the growth of the brain until something suddenly happened within the humanoid mind to produce a blinding, irradiating thing called consciousness that next to the kindred spirit of the ape would seem like a super-mind? Imagine the profound shock to the proto-anthropoid mind to suddenly pass through the door of self-awareness to behold an inner galaxy of rarefied knowledge and a potential knowability well beyond his normal range of comprehension, comparable perhaps to stumbling unexpectedly upon a hall of mirrors? The knowledge—indeed the responsibility—would have been too much to bear. Do we want to rely on the devotion of modern science to produce an answer to these questions based on purely empirical evidence? Do we want consciousness, which according to modern science finds its cardinal mode of expression in higher levels of mind, imagination and emotion, to be determined exclusively by the subterranean sense data and the matter substantiating the activity of the brain? Clearly, some people do.

(((

THE MIND, and its pervasive consciousness, is the one intangible reality that modern science does not fully comprehend and cannot control because it has not succeeded in measuring its elusive parameters and it does not dare to deny its existential presence.[7] Perhaps therein lies its determination to reduce the essence of man's humanity to its lowest common denominator in the ashes of purely physical matter in order to avoid the problem of coming to terms scientifically with an inviolable mystery.

The traditions do not say precisely what the mind or consciousness is. Instead, they state what the mind, and its higher counterpart the intellect, can accomplish. The religions resort to traditional images and universal symbols to clarify the difficult but important metaphysical concepts that everyone needs to comprehend, at least in principle. In one of the earliest traditional sources of Taoism in ancient China, Chuang Tzu, in his work entitled *The Book of Chuang Tzu*, refers to consciousness in this way:

> What I mean by the expression 'having good ears' does not concern the faculty of hearing the external objects (*t'a*). It concerns only hearing one's own 'self' (*tzu*). What I mean by the expression 'having good eyes' does not concern seeing the external objects. It concerns only seeing one's own 'self'.[8]

In this context, 'seeing one's own self' is a self-intuition that recalls what the Zen Buddhists call 'seeing one's [real] nature', a process that serves as a prelude and initiation to the experience of the higher consciousness that reflects not the individual self but the Supreme Self.

---

7. There is some considerable irony in the fact that what actually drives the scientific inquiry forward, namely the human mind in search of the true nature of reality, slips through the fingers of curious scientists and escapes their grasp precisely because they refuse to acknowledge its metaphysical origin and supra-natural source.

8. Quoted in *The Unanimous Tradition*, ed., Ranjit Fernando (Colombo: The Sri Lanka Institute of Traditional Studies, 1991), p 51.

In the Quran, Allah is identified as the All-Seeing (*al-basir*) as well as the All-Knowing (*al-alim*), these being the two counterpoints, and the balance if you will, of a comprehensive and complete consciousness, namely a knowledge with insight and an intuitive vision based on the essential knowledge of God. In the words of Coomaraswamy, this presence of mind is a 'point without extension' and a 'moment without duration', transcending time and place with its intuitive knowledge of the higher consciousness of God, of which man is a mirror reflection. The concept of both seeing and knowing reflects a vision of self and a knowledge of God that raises the context of consciousness above the earthly domain with its suggestion of a creative power greater capable of being assimilated into humanity as an operative faculty of perception and self-awareness.

In traditional literature, the symbol of the 'eye' has often been employed to represent the knowing Transcendent Self that extends beyond the limited human ego and the expression of the self as far as the outer reaches of the stars. The American transcendentalist Ralph Waldo Emerson touches upon this idea in his journals: 'Standing on bare ground,' he says, 'my head bathed by the blithe air and uplifted into infinite space, all mean egotism vanishes. I become a transparent eyeball; I am nothing, I see all; the currents of the Universal Being circulate through me; I am part or parcel of God.'[9] The transparent eyeball becomes an expression to denote the experience of the miracle of consciousness that sees and knows, reflecting not the contents of thought, but the channel through which the process of knowing passes. Through knowledge and vision, humans are able to take leave of their individual nothingness and transcend themselves into a container of the Supreme Consciousness. Through the mind's eye, humans are able to re-enact the qualities of God within the conscious mind of man.

If the universal consciousness enters humans through the mind, then it takes up residence in the heart, dwelling within as the 'eye' of the heart (*'ayn al-qalb*) and reflected within the intellect as a perfected and universal knowledge embodied as the 'eye' of certainty

9. As quoted in Loren Eiseley's *The Star Thrower*, p 211.

(*'ayn al-yaqin*).[10] The Quran identifies three levels of knowledge that lead ultimately to a confirmed certainty of the truth itself. The first degree of knowledge is the knowledge of the mind, character-ized in one Quranic verse as *certain knowledge* [*ilm al-yakin* (102:5)]. This represents the onslaught of a certainty that comes about through the normal course of logic and reasoning of the mind reminiscent of what humanity has achieved during these times in terms of scientific discovery and technological achieve-ment. This is balanced by the certainty that results from the 'eye of certainty' or alternatively translated 'the certainty of seeing' (*'ayn al-yaqin* [102:7]), in which man obtains a knowledge based on what he actually sees with his own eyes. Ultimately, the final degree of knowing results in what the Quran calls the 'certainty of the Truth' (*al haqq al yaqin* [69:51]), a certainty that lies within the 'seat' of man's intelligence—namely the heart of man—as 'the conscious eye' and the 'certainty of truth' that cannot be denied.

The traditional concept of consciousness embodies within its vision the many levels and modes of expression that the word implies. This includes a state of mind that is characteristically human rather than animal, an active and reflective thinking process that negotiates its way through all thoughts and impressions, a multi-tiered and multi-angled sense of awareness, a direct con-sciousness of self, a defining mode of self-expression, vast realms of imagination and emotion, the force of a free will, the living pres-ence of mind, and the power to objectify subjective experience into an objective knowledge. Ultimately, this 'spirit of mind' arrives at the final abode and resting place known as spiritual consciousness.

As the center of knowledge, human consciousness processes all incoming knowledge within a framework of spatial and temporal events that find their extension and meaning, not to mention their actual reality, within its trans-temporal and trans-spatial setting. Without such a center, the reality of this world would seem to enjoy an independent existence in its own right and have no extension beyond its physical, spatial and temporal truth. In other words, in separating the physical from the metaphysical essence, the reality of

10. In Hinduism, it recalls the frontal eye of Shiva.

the physical world would have the objectivity found in the trans-substantiating quality of physical matter amounting to a dust-to-ashes approach to the philosophy of life. Instead, the power of human consciousness promises us more by permitting people to examine the contents of the mind within a framework of reality that substantiates and then transcends the three dimensional structure of this world.

As the center of objectivity, human consciousness processes incoming knowledge within a frame of reference that is independent of the reason and ratiocination of the mind. As a mode of objectivity, consciousness is 'vertical' to the constant stream of thoughts, emotions, and desires that are mental, sensory, psychic and emotional and that provide the contents that the mind must evaluate and deal with. We are not just our brain and our mind in their sensorial and cognitive mode, for in claiming to know things, the brain is an instrument and the mind a vehicle for knowing only the superficial aspect of a questionable reality that is externalized and peripheral with respect to our inmost being and with respect to experience that we know to be beyond the purely physical manifestation of life.

As the center of transcendence, human consciousness serves as a bridge between worlds. It processes all incoming knowledge within a framework of higher realities that are based on the intuitive knowledge of God and that are experienced as sacred sentiments and higher emotions. What commences as a mindfulness of individuality that allows the mind to become aware of itself without being limited to the boundaries of the body reaches far beyond the physical organs of the brain and the mind to become a center of irradiation that opens onto the self that knows things intuitively and with a certainty. In an external world that is full of mystery, uncertainty and doubt, our inmost being becomes our one absolute certainty whose existence and whose reality we cannot dispute or deny. Our intuitive awareness of the inner self is the very starting-point and *modus operandi* of our self-consciousness. It represents the apogee of our humanness and the birthmark of the Divine Being

Behind the face of humanity lie an inward reality and a condition of knowability that we cannot actually measure or observe, but that we know exists by virtue of our experience of its enduring presence and the power of its consequences. I have it without which this work would not be possible; you have it, otherwise you never would have gotten this far in the reading; indeed, everyone has it without which they could not function as men and women within the world since it distinguishes who men and women are as human beings within a human society. We may not know what it is precisely, but we feel its process working within us as a higher reality descended upon our existential world, a reality that finds its origin and source in the knowledge of God. When opened to its fullest consciousness, it will ultimately turn humanity into a human revelation and a living source of knowledge.

In the end, the power of our human consciousness brings us face to face with ourselves and will lead us into the next age of humanity. Through the power of the inward eye of consciousness, we can identify ourselves, not in terms of physical matter and not in a precarious alliance with a purely human reason to negotiate its way through the impenetrable mysteries of life. Only the ill-defined and unexplained presence of consciousness that lies behind the symbolic human countenance will give us the prescience and temerity of mind to resolve the fundamental mystery that lies at the core of our existential experience of life. Only the knowledge of the self will open the invisible doorway of our being, a doorway that once opened becomes the 'sun door' to a transcending and trans-luminescent world. By passing through that door, modern-day humans will advance beyond the reality that they now know, in order to arrive at a reality that they will come to know as the true origin and ultimate source of knowledge in the Spirit of God and His abiding Presence.

AFTERWORD

NOTES FROM THE EDGE

WE HAVE COME A LONG WAY from reflecting upon the divine act of creation and the origin of the space/time continuum. Along the way, we have leafed through the book of nature and attempted to read the messages of the signs and symbols of the natural order that reflect the higher realities of a supernatural order. Finally, we arrived at an introspective look behind the open face of man whose contemporary mask we lifted to express some thoughts on the mystery of humanity's inner nature and the miracle of human consciousness.

We have come a long way because these seemingly disparate points of reference give the initial impression of being all too remote from our immediate experience, while at the same time they are infinitely close to all that we hold of value and consequence in our lives. We have explored a variety of frontiers that have led from the near horizon of the self to the distant horizon of the universe in order to examine and hold to the light what we already know as fact and what we need know as truth. What unites these seemingly disparate reflections concerning the true sources of knowledge is none other than the knowledge of God and the presence of His Abiding Spirit.

Intrusive questions still persist, however, and refuse to let us rest in holy peace. Do we as 'modern' individuals have the right to speculate upon these enigmatic ideas? The answer must be a definitive *yes*, for we have an obligation to come to terms with our origins, our meaning, and our ultimate end unless we want to risk misunderstanding ourselves, our true identity, and our role in the human narrative. Do we as individuals have the right to characterize and define these concepts solely within the human order? The answer must be and is a definitive *no* for ultimately their veracity and meaning originate beyond the realm of man's human consciousness and their reality exists as an independent truth outside of, indeed in spite of, man.

In addition, following upon this *yes* and *no*, we hear another question that echoes in the background of these pages like distant thunder: Why? Why should we be concerned with an 'event' that took place billions of years ago and worry about 'realities' that seem beyond our grasp? For modern science, the answer seems to be— apart from the more noble reason of searching for a 'theory of everything' that would explain the natural world—the discovery of irrefutable proof that the creation theory and thus the belief in a Supreme Deity is wrong and modern science is right. For the traditions, the motivation for re-exhuming the ground knowledge of our creation and first origins along with the divine revelation that substantiates that knowledge lies in the desire to identify the authentic sources of knowledge that alone can verify the true nature of Reality.

We have endeavored to emphasize the importance of identifying the true sources of knowledge precisely because the traditional sources of knowledge, in the form of revelation, nature and man, have been reduced in modern times to unrecognizable facsimiles of themselves, even though in their true manifestation they disclose knowledge that would not otherwise be known. Revelation no longer serves as the divine disclosure and sacred speech of the Divinity; nature no longer reflects the knowledge and living presence of God through the intelligent design of the natural order; and finally humanity no longer descends 'from above' as the symbol and reflection in human form of the divine qualities and attributes, but rather ascends 'from below' through an evolution of organic form that leads his evolution and development through a fantastic, transspecies adventure that passes through simian and humanoid forms before finally arriving at the reality of a 'thinking' and 'ethical' human.

In many ways, the writing of this book has been like taking a journey to the edge—to thresholds and potential gateways leading to a renewed understanding—of revelation, of nature, and of humanity, in order to uncover the essential knowledge in a variety of forms of natural revelation that must be the inevitable consequence of the kind of being we are. We commenced our reflections at that moment just before the creation of the universe, on the threshold of time when the primordial point emerged and came into being to become the universal manifestation of the cosmos. We noted that modern science is reluctant to go outside the parameters of its competence and therefore denies the ever-present 'eternity' that lies outside the time-space continuum of the created universe. On the contrary, the traditions suggest that this continuum lies within the existing moment of eternity as a temporal event in an atemporal setting. To gaze into eternity is to journey innerly to the edge by looking through the axis of space and time. To believe in its eternal possibility is to journey beyond the distant horizon.

Through a profound reversal of human fortune, we now exist on the periphery and edge of nature rather than live within its comforting presence and profit from its enduring meaning. We no longer read the messages that the animate and inanimate symbols of nature convey, and we no longer understand the monumental role that nature plays in providing the backdrop and setting of the earthly endeavor. Today, we study nature, not to understand the secret of its revealing mystery and not to enrich ourselves with its fundamental beauty and sacred ambiance, but rather to discover her secrets purely for our own dubious purposes and to gain control over her dark forces for our own questionable ends. Never has the danger for people today been so great and never has the fascination with nature's potential power been as strong as now, when scientists have succeeded in uncovering mysteries that they never expected to confront in their wildest dreams. They see beyond their own limited horizon to the end of the universe some 15 billion light years away. They listen at the end of a wire to the whispering of galaxies. Yet in travelling to places that they will never visit in person, they still remain on the edge of nature, analyzing its physical properties without intuiting its inner message, observing from the edge of the forest as it were, from the outside looking in, within reach of a spiritual borderland they are unwilling to cross over and enter.

Finally, the modern psyche has abandoned the gateway to the inner self and now lives on the edge of a complete life experience. In ignoring the revelation that lies as knowledge of self in reflection of the Supreme Self, the modern mentality now understands itself to be merely a finite, corporeal being who abides by the strength of its own physical and mental resources. At first glance, this may seem like a formidable position worthy of any titan. Scientists have sent space probes into the outer reaches of the solar system and have put a foot on the moon. They have uncovered and are now examining the genetic code of DNA, bringing within their manipulative reach the very alphabet of life. They hold the forces of the atom within their grasp like a spear and they explore the human brain searching for a source and explanation for the defining quality of their own consciousness. Yet, they are still not satisfied with what they have accomplished and continue to yearn for the meaning and the truth that eludes their inquiry.

Two final considerations bear mentioning within this context. Firstly, modern science need not necessarily close itself off from other levels of perception that may shed light on its professed objective to find a 'theory of everything' that can serve as a universal knowledge to identify the true nature of reality. The knowledge we seek in the distant regions of outer space and the answers we endeavor to find within the cellular life of the human body may lie, not in the speculation of distant galaxies and the fascination with swarming microbes, but in an alternative medium that lies outside the spectrum of a purely physical reality.

Secondly, in the pursuit of a scientific inquiry since the time of the Renaissance, the scientific community has developed and brought to a rarefied level of expertise the five human senses through which scientists have explored nearly every aspect of quantifiable nature, uncovering along the way the very seams of the world. Humanity sees and listens, but their seeing and listening need not encompass merely the physical plane of existence. There also exist higher perceptions that transcend the purely physical and corporeal experiences of man, amounting to an intuition and a knowledge that begins as faith in the one God and ends as certitude of the one Reality.

Humanity is destined to know, because the hint of the essential knowledge and the presentiment of an answer lie in the very cells of the human body. Moreover, they want to know because their mind, imagination, emotions and formidable human will also exist within their beings to serve as the higher faculties of insight and perception. Beyond the universe of distant galaxies and the microscopic world of DNA lies an inner universe of sacred intelligence and spiritual intuition that shapes the perception and innermost senses of humanity. We have travelled vast distances across the millennia from primitive caves and distant jungles to modern metropolises and sophisticated environments because we are at heart an observer and a listener; but we have not traversed those distances to look into the mirrors and miracles of modern science only to find the first origin and final end of the physical world.

Humanity is an observer and a listener, but we are also dreamers of dreams that come true. We have traversed the millennia and broken through boundaries that control all other forms of life. We have crossed the vast distances that separate primitive man from modern man. We have the capacity to dream, not only of what lies in our immediate future, but also of what lies beyond the near horizon of the self and the distant horizon of the world.

As observer and listener, we study and examine ourselves and our world with a view to uncovering our deepest secrets. As dreamer of dreams, we search far and wide for a metaphysical principle with the explanatory power of a revelation. As seekers in search of the truth, however, we may learn that in discovering the true nature of ourselves and the world, we will also come to realize the knowledge of the Transcendent Being who disclosed His Mystery in the sacred words of revelation, in the symbolic forms of nature, and in the evocative image of a conscious human being.

www.ingramcontent.com/pod-product-compliance
Lightning Source LLC
Chambersburg PA
CBHW021058090426
42738CB00006B/397